Battenberg and Other Tape Laces

TECHNIQUES, STITCHES AND DESIGNS

by

The Butterick Publishing Co.

DOVER PUBLICATIONS, INC., *New York*

Published in Canada by General Publishing Company, Ltd., 30 Lesmill Road, Don Mills, Toronto, Ontario.
Published in the United Kingdom by Constable and Company, Ltd.

Battenberg and Other Tape Laces: Techniques, Stitches and Designs, first published by Dover Publications, Inc., in 1988, is an abridged republication of *Modern Lace-Making: Advanced Studies,* published by The Butterick Publishing Co. (Limited), London and New York, in 1901. The section "Method of Cleaning Fine Lace," one page of advertising and twenty photographs have been omitted; see Publisher's Note for further information.

Manufactured in the United States of America
Dover Publications, Inc.
31 East 2nd Street
Mineola, N.Y. 11501

Library of Congress Cataloging-in-Publication Data

Hadley, Sara.
    [Modern lace-making]
    Battenberg and other tape laces : techniques, stitches, and designs / by the Butterick Publishing Co.
        p.   cm.
    Reprint. Originally published: Modern lace-making. London ; New York : Butterick Pub. Co., 1901.
    ISBN 0-486-25643-X (pbk.)
    1. Lace and lace making.   I. Butterick Publishing Company. II. Title.   III. Title: Tape laces.
    TT800.H13   1988
    746.2′2—dc19   87-35415
                                                           CIP

Publisher's Note

The end of the nineteenth and the beginning of the twentieth century saw the rise of a new form of needlework. This work, called modern point lace, or merely modern lace, attempted to duplicate the laces of the seventeenth and eighteenth centuries, and was accomplished by basting machine-made braid or cord to a pattern, sewing the braid together securely where it touched, and filling the spaces with lace stitches. The resulting lace was known by various names—Modern Flemish, Honiton, Bruges, etc.—depending on the type of braid and the filling stitches used. A wide variety of braids, cords, buttonholed rings and lace appliqués was available, enabling workers to copy almost every type of antique lace. Purists derided these imitations, considering them inferior and not "real" laces at all. Nevertheless, their popularity was enormous, and, when done with skill, the work was extremely beautiful. Unlike most earlier forms of lace, modern laces were made primarily by amateurs, rather than as a commercial endeavor.

In America, one of the most popular forms of this work was called Battenberg Lace, also known as Royal Battenberg. This was originally among the heaviest of the modern laces, although lighter braids were developed for it. Because Battenberg was so well known, the term is now used to describe any of the laces made in this way.

The popularity of modern lace was encouraged by the needlework magazines of the day, which published numerous patterns and instructions for collars, handkerchiefs, edgings, tablecloths, doilies, runners and other accessories, often combining the lace with embroidery or other needlework techniques.

This book, published at the height of the modern-lace craze, was prepared with the assistance of Sara Hadley, a well-known American lacemaker who was said to be the inventor of Royal Battenberg Lace. Miss Hadley provided the information and the designs for the book, and all of the patterns, braids, cords, rings and appliqués could be ordered directly from her. This edition contains all of the instruction pages from the original, but several of the photographs have been omitted because of their poor quality. One page of advertising has been left out and we have eliminated the section "Method of Cleaning Fine Lace," because several of the methods have since been found to be harmful to the lace.

By the beginning of the First World War, the vogue for modern lace had died out. It disappeared from the pages of the magazines and much of the beautiful lace made in earlier years was relegated to the attic. Today, however, lace and lacemaking of all kinds are enjoying a comeback. While our choice of braids may be somewhat more limited than when this book first appeared, many types of lace braid can be purchased wherever lacemaking supplies are sold. If you have difficulty locating materials, they may be ordered by mail from Lacis, 2982 Adeline Street, Berkeley, California 94703.

All of the techniques needed and the stitches used in making laces of this type are illustrated and explained in these pages, but perhaps the book's greatest value lies in the large number of lace samples shown. Even though we can no longer order full-size patterns for them from Miss Hadley's lacemaking establishment, the almost 200 designs illustrated are sure to provide a wealth of inspiration to today's lacemaker.

CONTENTS

"A needle, though it be but small and slender,
Is truly both a maker and a mender
 .   .   .   .   . A needle is an instrument
Of profit, pleasure, and of ornament."
—JOHN TAYLOR.

"Silently as a dream the fabric rose."
—COWPER.

"Spun from the cobweb fashion of the times."
—AKENSIDE.

AFTERNOON TEA-CLOTH OF RUSSIAN LACE.

Modern Lace-Making:

ADVANCED STUDIES.

MODERN LACE as illustrated throughout this book is of recent origin and does not include those varieties made over cushions and pillows with bobbins and originated hundreds of years ago. To make those costly laces of foreign commerce requires workers trained from childhood. Pillow Lace, while exceedingly dainty and pretty, is not adaptable to the workers of to-day. The materials and implements are costly and the work intricate; the number of bobbins necessitated by one single pattern frequently exceeding fifty. This causes bewilderment, except to an experienced worker, and the progress is so slow that few care to take it up.

The designs here illustrated are all direct reproductions of hand-made modern laces and may be made by any one who is clever with her needle and has a taste for such work. They are chiefly new designs of older characters, or combinations of several styles of laces composed of various braids and stitches.

Modern Lace is made with braids, cords, rings (see pages 65, 66, 67, 68 and 69) and threads, from designs drawn on muslin. On pages 41 to 64 of this book will be found engravings of and explicit directions for making all the necessary stitches used in Modern Lace, together with much valuable information as to the materials required. The complete art is set forth in these pages which also contain a large number of designs for Edgings, Insertions, Collars, Handkerchiefs, Parasol Covers, Centre-Pieces, Doilies, Napery, Fans, Lingerie, and Infants' Caps, Bibs, etc.

Modern Lace is classed as follows: Modern Flemish, Modern Venetian Point, Royal Battenberg or Old English Point, Renaissance, Needle Point, Honiton, Ideal Honiton, Duchesse or Princess, Bruges, Limoges, and Point Lace. Of these all are more or less familiar to our readers with the exception of the first two named.

Modern Flemish lace is the invention of Sara Hadley, of 34 West 22nd street, New York, a lace-maker known to both continents as the originator of Royal Battenberg Lace. Venetian Point Lace until lately was considered an antique. A fragment of old Venetian Point from the Coliseum at Rome gave Miss Hadley the idea from which grew Modern Venetian Point, the beauty of which is beyond all question. This "fragment" of lace was made upon a foundation like that of drawn-work, undrawn threads forming the thick portions, and darning producing the open effects. In Modern Venetian Point the thick portions are all made stitch by stitch, forming a texture so like woven cloth that it is difficult to realize its real composition. There are many varieties of Venetian Point stitches (see page 48) and they are called into use in making Modern Venetian Point, the foundation of which is heavy linen threads wrought over with button-hole stitch. The detail is illustrated on page 81 of this book.

Realizing the beauty and durability of Venetian Point, Miss Hadley began and completed the Table-Cover shown on page 82 of this book. The climax of her idea, however, is not manifest in this piece of work. It was intended to have embroidered on each of the hand-made linen squares alternating with the lace ones the monogram or initials of a member of the family together with the date, and, possibly the crest or coat-of-arms. In this way the cover would become a valuable family heirloom.

The work is difficult because of its tediousness, but the latter will be understood by reference to page 81, where a square of the Point of nearly full size is shown. Every stitch in the whole square is made separately, with a pointless needle and fine linen thread.

The linen is coarse of mesh but very soft and is of a deep, rich cream tint, the Point also being carried out in the same coloring.

Aside from the use of Venetian Point just mentioned, it is especially suitable for centre-pieces, doilies, etc., to be used upon polished tables, the dark wood of which most advantageously displays its elegance. In church lace—that used upon altars, draperies, vestments, etc.—it has a sumptuous effect wholly in keeping with other surroundings.

Royal Battenberg lace is the most generally used of all the modern laces for table-centres, doilies, tidies, squares, borders, etc., and is followed in popularity by the more easily-made Renaissance. Battenberg designs have connecting bars wrought with button-hole stitch and picots, and frequently include cords, rings, buttons, etc., these additions being specially made for varying the general effects of Battenberg lace. Renaissance lace, however, is easily made, the only stitches employed being twisted connecting bars and spider-wheels or other flat stitches, with the braid connected here and there with worked rings, all of which render the lace lighter and less rich in effect. Occasionally an amateur will contend that there is no difference in these two laces, but an inspection of genuine Battenberg and Renaissance laces will at once convince even the casual observer that there is a very material difference.

Honiton, Point and Duchesse laces are those most seen in handkerchiefs, collars, fine doilies, edgings, etc.

Bruges lace is seen in collars, edgings, insertions, etc., and, made with Flemish lace braids, is exquisite for other purposes—yokes, bonnet and hat crowns, jacket-fronts, etc.

Ideal Honiton is eminently suitable for bureau-scarfs, doilies, centre-pieces, babies' pillow-slips, etc. The process of making it is described on page 41 of this book.

In making Modern Lace a lady need not feel that she is wasting time on something that is of little value. Every bit of lace so made is "real lace" and where is the woman who does not value the possession of real lace almost as much as she does a collection of jewels? And when made by herself why does not her "real lace" become doubly valuable, not only as her own handicraft, but something her children may cherish and pass on to the next generation? Modern Lace-Making is not mere fancy work—it is art.

The laces and designs illustrated, the stitches and the information contained in this book, were furnished by Sara Hadley, professional lace-maker of No. 34 West 22nd street, New York.

PLATE A.—APPLIQUÉ ORNAMENTS IN DUCHESSE AND POINT LACE.

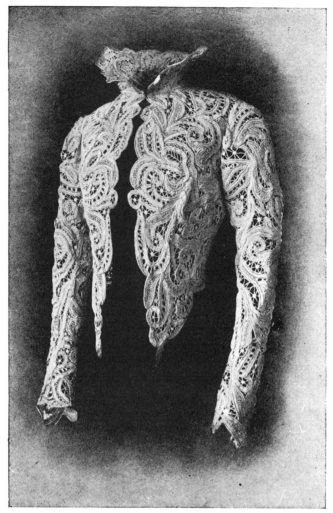

No. 1.—Ladies' Jacket in Russian Lace. (Front.)

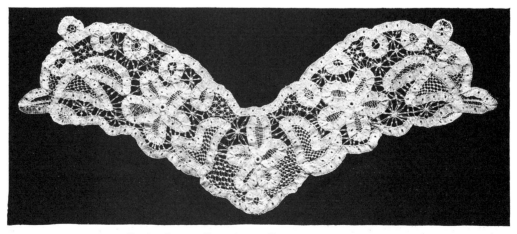

No. 2.—Bruges Lace Stock Collar. (Roman Style.)

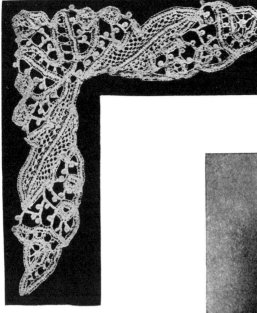

No. 3.—Napkin Medallion in
Battenberg Lace.

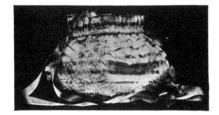

No. 4.—Opera Bag with Lace
Decoration.

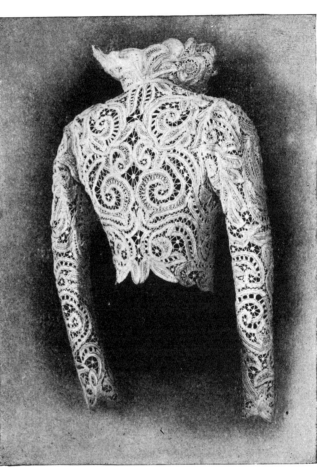

No. 5.—Ladies' Jacket in Russian Lace. (Back.)

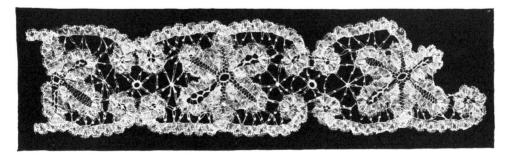

No. 6.—Bruges Lace Insertion.

No. 7.—Jabot Collar in Renaissance and Appliqué.

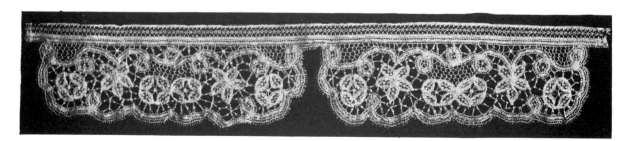

No. 8.—Princess Lace Turn-over Collar.

No. 9.—Renaissance Centre-Piece.

No. 10.—Needle-Book in Modern Lace.

No. 11.—Renaissance Edge.

No. 12.—Cream and Gold Lace Scarf.

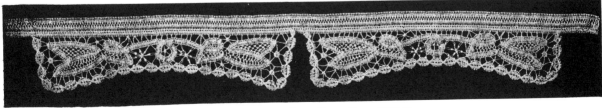

No. 13.—Princess Lace Turn-Over Collar.

13

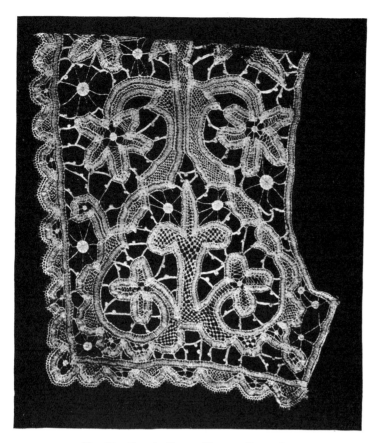

No. 14.—Baby's Cap in Modern Point Lace.

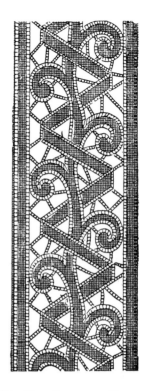

No. 15. — Design in Modern Lace.

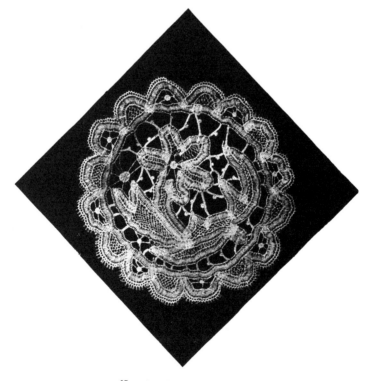

No. 16.—Crown for Baby's Cap.

No. 17.—Corset-Cover with Yoke of Modern Lace.

No. 18.—Bow-Knot in Russian Lace.

No. 19.—Point Lace Edging.

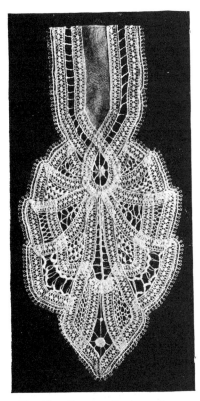

No. 20.—Barb in Princess Lace.

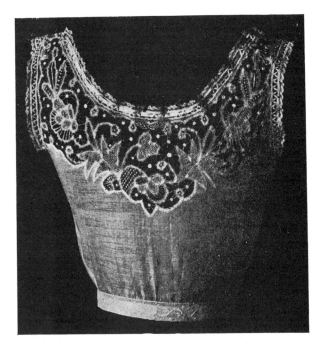

No. 21.—Lace Yoke Corset-Cover. (Back.)

No. 22.—BUTTERFLY SCARF IN POINT LACE.

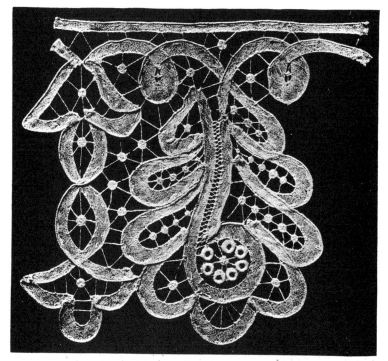

No. 23.—FLEMISH LACE EDGING.

No. 24.—Chiffonier Scarf of English Point.

No. 25.—Punch-Glass Doily of Point Lace and Lawn.

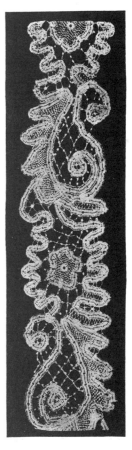

No. 26.—Bruges Lace
Insertion.

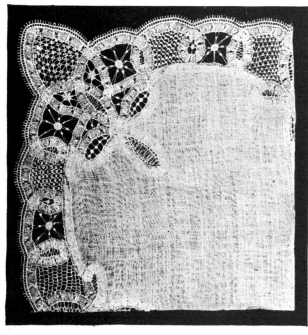

No. 27.—Handkerchief with Bruges Lace Border.

No. 28.—Honiton Leaf Appliqué.

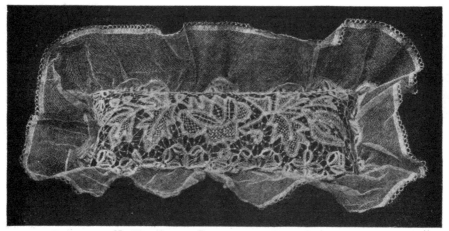

No. 29.—Oblong Pincushion in Point Lace.

No. 30.—Sideboard Scarf of Modern Lace.

No. 31.—Collar of Roman Lace.

No. 32.—Net Scarf in Honiton and Point.

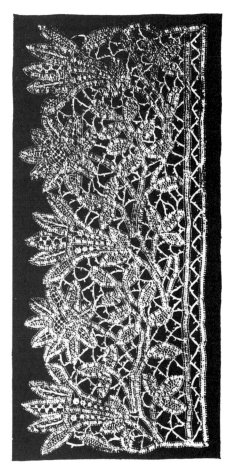

No. 33.—Battenberg Lace.

19

No. 34.—Scarf in Point and Honiton Appliqué.

No. 35.—Modern Lace Edging.

No. 36.—Five O'Clock Tea-Cloth of Cluny Lace.

No. 37.—Renaissance Lace Insertion.

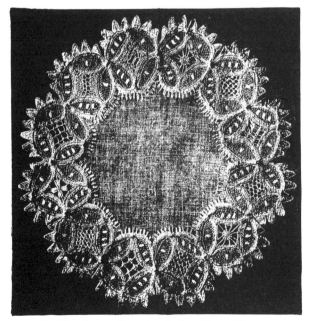

No. 38.—Ideal Honiton Finger-Bowl Doily.

No. 39.—Bruges Lace Tie.

No. 40. — Royal Battenberg Table-Centre.

No. 41. — Appliqué Spray in Honiton.

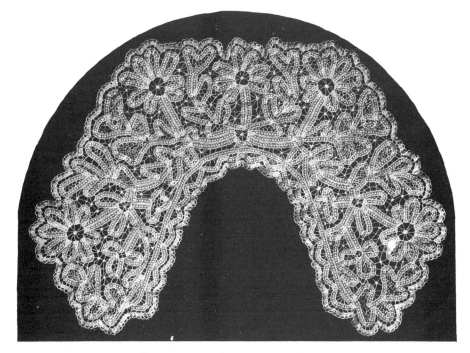

No. 42.—Ladies' Fancy Lace Collar.

No. 43.—Modern Venetian Point.

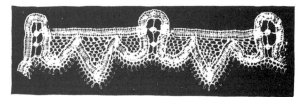

No. 44.—Point Lace Edge

No. 45.—Round Pincushion in Point Lace.

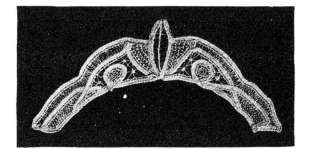

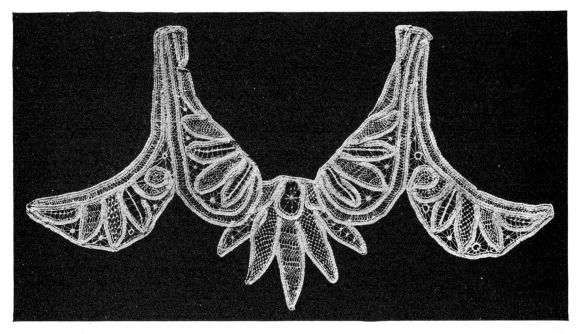

No. 46.—Waist Decoration in Russian Lace.

No. 47.—Flemish Lace in Rose Design.

24

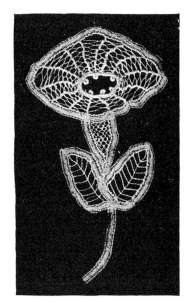

No 49. — Morning Glory Appliqué.

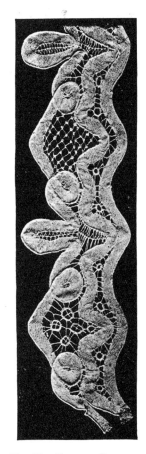

No. 48. — Battenberg Edging.

No. 50. — Flemish Insertion.

No. 51.—Coat Collar and Revers in Royal Battenberg

No. 52.—Point Lace Finger-Bowl Doily.

No. 53.—Chiffon Scarf in Needle Point.

26

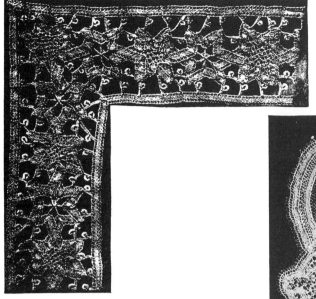

No. 54.—Battenberg Insertion for Napkin.

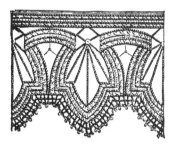

No. 55.—Modern Lace Edge.

No. 56. Point Lace Handkerchief with Honiton Appliqué.

No. 57.—Honiton and Point Lace Table–Centre.

27

No. 58.—Plate–Doily to Match Honiton and Point Table–Centre.

No. 59.—Point Lace Finger-Bowl Doily.

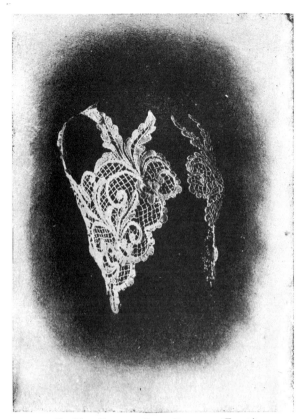

No. 61.—Fleur de lis Appliqué.

No 60.—Russian Lace Bolero. (Front.)

No. 62.—Collar Point of Honiton and Point Lace.

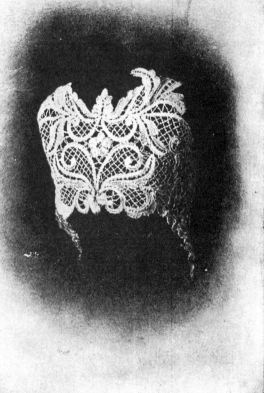

No. 63.—Russian Lace Bolero. (Back.)

29

No 64.—Stole Fichu of Bruges Lace.

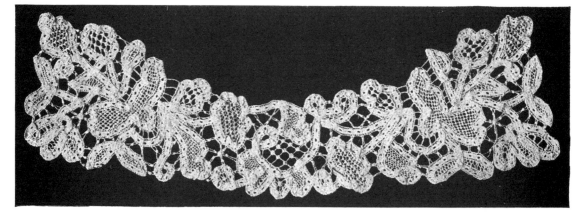

No. 65.—Stock Collar of Bruges Lace.

30

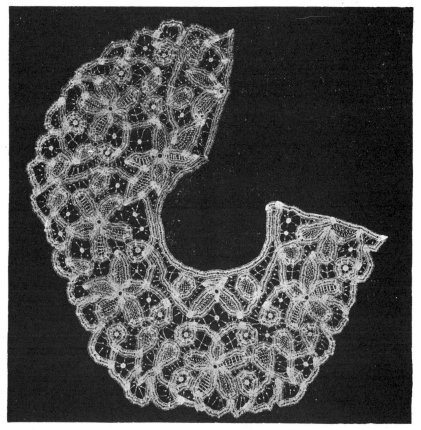

No. 66.—Ladies' Yoke of Bruges Lace.

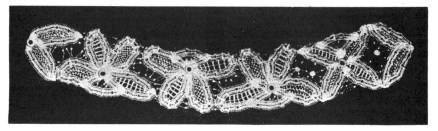

No. 67.—Bruges Lace Stock for Yoke.

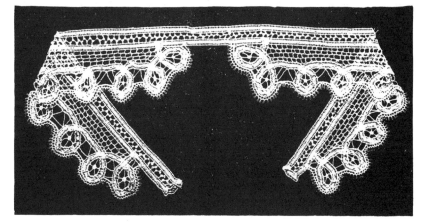

No. 68.—Turn-Over Collar of Point Lace.

31

No. 69.—Royal Battenberg Border for Table-Cloth.

No. 70.—Finger-Bowl Doily in Needle Point.

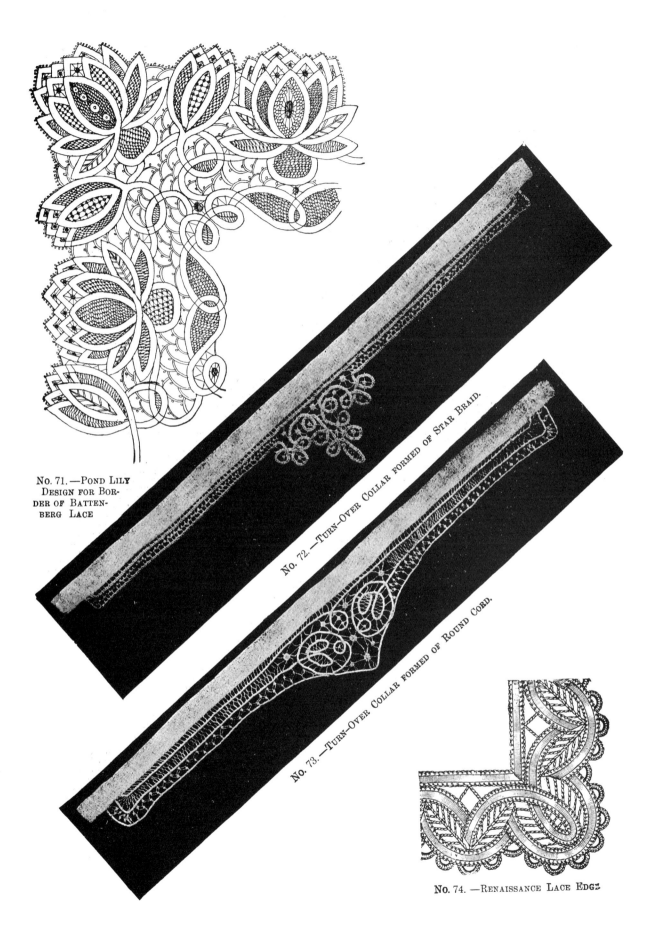

No. 71.—Pond Lily
Design for Bor-
der of Batten-
berg Lace

No. 72.—Turn-Over Collar formed of Star Braid.

No. 73.—Turn-Over Collar formed of Round Cord.

No. 74.—Renaissance Lace Edge

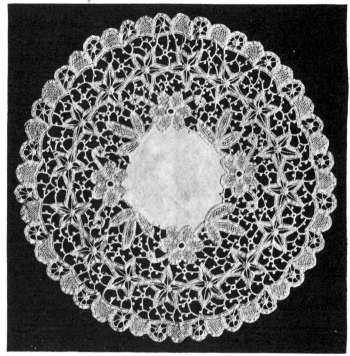

No. 75.—Plate Doily to Match Royal Battenberg Table-Centre.

No. 76.—Ladies' Stock with Modern
Lace Turn-Over and Tie-Ends.

No. 77.—Double Lace Butterfly.

No. 78.—Tea-Table Cloth in English Point.

No. 79.—Turn-Over Collar of Point Lace.

No. 80.—Point Lace Fan.

No. 81.—Finger-Bowl Doily in Royal Battenberg Lace.

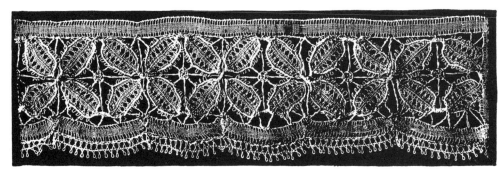

No. 82.—Honiton Lace Edging.

No. 83.—Fichu Collar
of Russian Lace.

No. 84.—Renaissance Table Centre.

No. 85.—Ladies' Turn-Over Collar of Honiton and Point Lace.

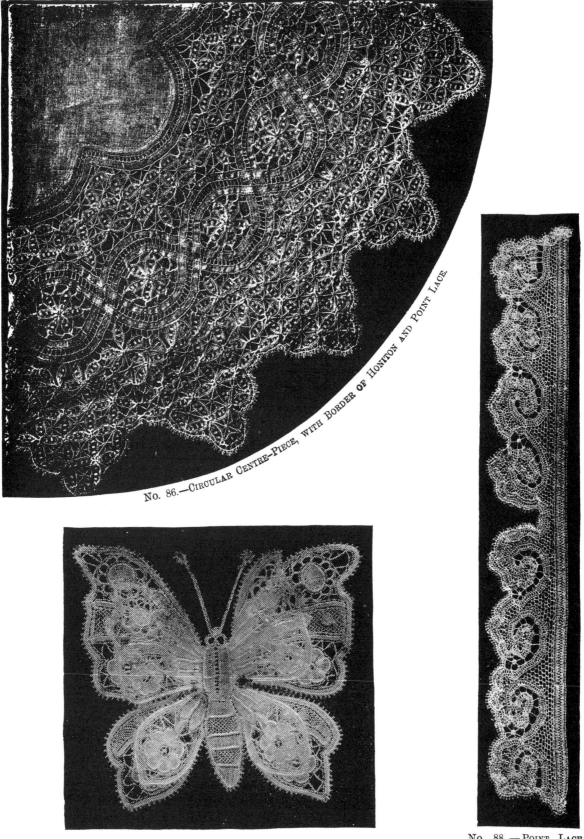

No. 86.—Circular Centre-Piece, with Border of Honiton and Point Lace.

No. 87.—Double Butterfly of Modern Lace.

No. 88. — Point Lace Turn-Over Collar.

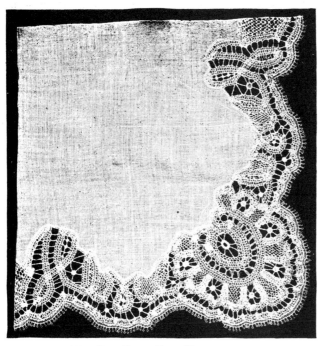

No. '89. —Point Lace Handkerchief.

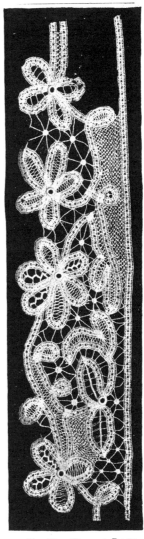

No. 91. —Bruges Lace Edging.

No. 90. —Point Lace Tie-End.

39

PLATE B.—APPLIQUÉ ORNAMENTS OF VALENCIENNES, POINT AND RUSSIAN LACE.

INSTRUCTIONS IN MODERN LACE MAKING.

MODERN LACES AND THE MATERIALS REQUIRED IN MAKING THEM.

ODERN LACES are classed as Modern Flemish, Modern Venetian Point, Honiton, Point, Needle-Point, Duchesse or Princess, Royal Battenberg or Old English Point, Bruges, Limoges, and Ideal Honiton; but all are made with various braids arranged in different patterns and connected by numerous kinds of stitches, many different stitches often appearing in one variety of lace. Many varieties of Modern Lace are developed by combining one or more of the kinds specified above.

The materials required in making Modern Lace are neither numerous nor expensive. The following is a complete list: Tracing linen, leather or glazed muslin, lace braids of various kinds, linen thread of proper textures or sizes, two or three sizes of needles (those without points are the best), a good thimble and a pair of sharp scissors.

For each kind of lace there is a special sort of braid in various patterns, as will be seen by referring to pages 65, 66, 67, 68 and 69, and the selection of the thread depends entirely upon the variety and quality of lace to be made. This selection should be left to the decision of the teacher or the skilled maker of laces, as she knows from experience the proper combination of materials. Thus, in making Honiton and point lace, thread in twelve different degrees of fineness is used; and as the braids also vary in size, the thread must always be adapted to the braid. For Battenberg lace the thread is in eight sizes, the finest being used only for "whipping curves" or drawing the edges into the outlines required. The other laces all have their special threads which will be designated by any lace-maker of whom inquiries are made.

Modern Flemish Lace is an entirely new product, originated and developed by Sara Hadley, of 34 West 22nd Street, New York, the well-known inventor of Royal Battenberg Lace. It is very quaint and attractive in design and, although very fine, not difficult to make, since all the animals, insects, etc., used in making it may be purchased in the shapes completely worked.

Modern Venetian Point is another new lace, as may be seen by referring to page 82 of this book, where a tea-cloth of Venetian Point and linen squares is portrayed. On page 81 may be seen an almost full-size square of the lace, together with a detail design in the same kind of work.

The "Ideal Honiton" is a lace made with fancy Honiton braid and wash-silk floss, and is exquisite for doilies, table and bureau scarfs and centre-pieces. The design is traced on fine linen lawn, the braid is then basted on, and fastened down with short and long button-hole stitches and a pointed edge of the same is added, after which the material is cut away from the scollops and from under the braid. The numerous illustrations of Ideal Honiton on these pages, perfectly disclose the method of making.

Designs sold by lace-makers are usually drawn upon glazed cloth, as this is flexible and much more agreeable to work upon than any other material. The cloth on which the design is drawn is, when the braid is arranged, basted to a foundation of leather, although smooth wrapping paper may be basted under the design and will furnish all the support that is necessary. In basting the braid, better results are obtained by basting at the outer edges for all curves, as seen in the first illustration on page 44; this prevents the braid from rolling up and distorting the design.

It must be remembered in making lace that the work, except in Venetian Point, is really wrong side out while in progress, so that it does not show its true beauty until finished and removed from the foundation or pattern. In Venetian Point, however, the work must be done on the right side, as the foundation is a single thread over which button-hole stitches are worked, and in these stitches others are worked. According to the braid and thread selected, these laces may be made of fairy-like fineness or of massive elegance—general results being dainty enough for the gown of a bride or sumptuous enough for the adornment of an altar.

Lace-making establishments will furnish designs of any width or shape desired, and will also originate designs for special articles for which there are only occasional calls; as not infrequently a handkerchief design is enlarged sufficiently to form a square or centre-piece for a table.

In filling in the spaces of any design or pattern, the worker may choose the stitches that please her best, if she does not like those accompanying the design she has selected or that has been sent her. She will find upon the following pages over a hundred specimens of stitches; and these, with the many designs of laces also given, should supply her with all the material and instruction necessary to aid her in the production of any of the varieties of Modern Lace.

FANCY BRAIDS, CORDS, RINGS, BUTTONS, AND ANIMAL, INSECT AND FLORAL ORNAMENTS, MEDALLIONS, ETC.

In making Modern Lace, the various kinds require appropriate braids. There are several classes of these braids—those for Battenberg, Renaissance, Marie Antoinette and Bruges laces, those for Honiton, Point, Duchesse or Princess, Ideal Honiton and Modern Flemish. Each class of braids contains many designs and widths, and a large number of them, together with various cords, buttons and rings, also used, are illustrated on pages 65 to 69.

BRAIDS AND CORDS.

The braids and cords illustrated are all made of pure linen thread, and, according to the fancy, lace including them may be heavy or light. Royal Battenberg lace, as originated, was heavy—in some cases massive; but at present many lighter varieties are made, as will be surmised upon an inspection of the braids used for its manufacture, which are represented on the pages mentioned. These and all other braids are given in their actual widths. The numbers opposite the specimens are simply for convenience in ordering, if the order is sent to the lady whose name is mentioned on page 7 and elsewhere in this book; but in ordering from other lace-makers or manufacturers of braids these numbers will be of little use, as every lace-maker or manufacturer has his or her own individual identifications for materials. Almost any of the braids, or those very similar, may be found at large fancy stores; but in buying them at such stores be careful to get *linen* braids, as cotton braids do not make pretty lace neither do they launder well. In ordering these braids from other lace-makers or from fancy stores, it will be necessary to forward the illustration of the kind wanted, as the braids cannot be described with sufficient accuracy to obtain the desired varieties. Some are sold by the yard, some by the dozen yards and others by the piece.

The Point and Honiton braids are much daintier in texture than the Battenberg braids. Of this class of braids (see pages 67, 68 and 69), are made the plain Honiton and Point laces, and the braids for these two laces combined produce Princess or Duchesse lace—a creation whose beauty fully entitles it to its royal name. On page 66 at Nos. 67 to 85 may also be seen braids for the new Modern Flemish lace.

The braids seen at Nos. 211 to 227, page 69, are those which are used in making Ideal Honiton lace, represented in other parts of the book. This is a very pretty lace, and, as before mentioned, is very appropriate for doilies, squares and bureau scarfs.

The cords seen at Nos. 27 to 35, page 65, are used in making Battenberg and Russian laces, and greatly increase the beauty of the work in addition to forming a distinctive species of lace. After the ordinary lace is worked with braid, the cord, in any size desired, may be used to follow one edge of the design.

RINGS AND BUTTONS.

The rings and buttons illustrated at Nos. 36 to 48, page 65, are made throughout of linen thread in layers of button-hole stitches worked over a foundation ring of wound thread and are sold by the dozen or gross. Intelligent lace-makers can, by an inspection of the illustration and an observance of the hint given in this paragraph, make them for themselves or customers with no difficulty.

ANIMAL, INSECT AND FLORAL ORNAMENTS, MEDALLIONS, ETC.

The ornaments seen on pages 9 and 40, are also the invention of the clever lace-maker already mentioned. They may be obtained singly, in sets, or by the dozen or gross at her establishment, or most of them may be made by any lace-maker, amateur or professional, as the engravings perfectly show the method necessary to their construction.

Many of these ornaments applied, may be seen at some of the engravings of Modern Flemish and other laces in various parts of the book.

ACTUAL SIZES OF THE LACES AND ARTICLES ILLUSTRATED.

It will be readily understood that it is impossible to give all of the designs and illustrations of the articles represented in this book in their full size. For the benefit of those who do not know what the sizes are, we would say that tumbler or punch glass doilies are usually from three and a half to four inches in diameter; finger-bowl doilies are from four to five inches across, while other doilies are from six to eight inches in diameter, or of the dimensions required by the dishes or articles they are to rest under or cover. Sizes may also be governed by individual taste.

Centre-pieces are from twenty-four inches square (or in diameter) to any size necessary to fit the table they are to be used upon.

Edgings and articles for wear are of such widths and dimensions as may be decided by personal taste. Every pattern in the book can be adapted by either a clever amateur or a professional lace-maker, to any size required. Many of the designs can be used as given.

SAMPLER OF MODERN LACE STITCHES.

METHODS OF BASTING BRAID TO A DESIGN.

DIAGRAM SHOWING HOW TO BASTE BRAID TO A DESIGN.

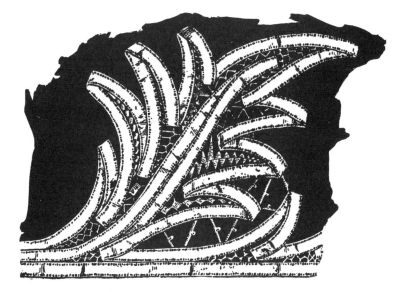

METHOD OF REVERSING THE BRAID.

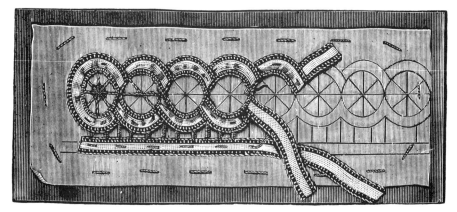

METHOD OF LAPPING THE BRAID.

(A Description of the Methods appears upon Page 41.)

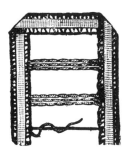

No. 1.—Sorrento or Plain
Twisted Bars.

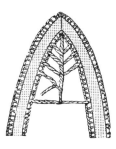

No. 2.—Sorrento Bars
in Leaf Form.

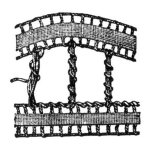

No. 3.—Double Twisted
Bars.

No. 4.—Sorrento Wheel
or Spider.

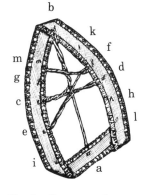

No. 5.—Detail of Sorrento
Wheel or Spider.

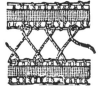

No. 6.—Plain
Russian Stitch.

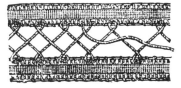

No. 7.—Double Russian
Stitch.

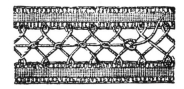

No. 8.—Russian Stitch with
Bar.

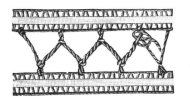

No. 9.—Twisted Russian Stitch.

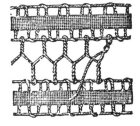

No. 10.—Column
Stitch.

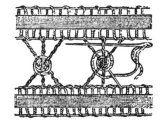

No. 11.—Rosette
Bars.

STITCHES USED IN MAKING MODERN LACE.

As in all fancy work which has a set of foundation stitches peculiar to it that may be varied according to the proficiency and ingenuity of the maker, so has Modern Lace a series of primary stitches from which may be evolved many others. A large number of illustrations of stitches, some of which are primary or foundation stitches, while others are combinations, are here presented, with full instructions for making; and the entire series given will make perfectly plain to the student the ease with which she may combine or invent stitches, when those of the design she has to work are not to her liking. Point de Bruxelles or net stitch is the main foundation stitch. The simplest is the Sorrento Bar.

Nos. 1 AND 2.—SORRENTO BARS.—Each of the bars is worked from right to left, a straight thread being carried across and fastened securely with a stitch. The return consists of a simple twist under and over the straight thread several times, according to the breadth, and these bars are repeated singly or in groups of two or three and four in the large spaces. The thread is sewed carefully over the braid in passing from one spot to another.

No. 3.—DOUBLE TWISTED BARS.—Several bars are worked in one space with the simple twist worked loosely so that the bars may be seen underneath. This mode of joining is particularly desirable when the spaces suddenly increase or decrease in distance.

Nos. 4 AND 5.—SORRENTO WHEEL.—This is worked by fastening the thread in the pattern to be filled up, as indicated by the letters. Fasten it first to the place a, then at place b, carrying it back to the middle of the first formed bar by winding it round; fasten again at c, carrying it back again to the centre by winding it around the bar, and so on to all the letters; then work over and under the bars thus formed.

Nos. 6, 7 AND 8.—RUSSIAN STITCH.—No. 6 is a fine herring-bone stitch. The single herring-bone or cross-stitch, in very narrow spaces, must be worked into the braid. No. 7 represents the double cross-stitch consisting of two lines lying over each other. No. 8 gives the same stitch, fastened by a button-hole stitch made across it.

No. 9.—TWISTED RUSSIAN STITCH.—This stitch is used to fill in narrow spaces where great lightness of effect is desired, and is usually seen along the sides of insertions and the tops of edgings. Plain point d'Alençon is worked over and under in bars in a sort of herring-bone pattern, and a twisted stitch is made as seen in the engraving, by twisting the thread three times around each bar and knotting it at the angles as pictured. The effect is similar to one of the drawn-work hemstitches.

No. 10.—COLUMN STITCH.—These bars are worked, like the herring-bone stitch, along both sides, but are twisted in coming back so as to form the columns shown in the illustration.

No. 11.—ROSETTE BARS.—These bars have a pretty effect in joining; they belong to the class of rosettes or spinning-stitches.

Nos. 12, 13 AND 14.—POINT DE BRUXELLES, BRUSSELS POINT OR SINGLE NET STITCH.—Among the stitches used in lace-making is Point de Bruxelles or Brussells Point. It is simply a button-hole stitch worked loosely, and it must be done with regularity, as the beauty of the work depends almost wholly upon the evenness of the stitches. Brussels Point is occasionally used as an edge, but is more frequently seen in rows worked back and forth to fill in spaces, or as a ground work. The illustrations clearly represent the methods of making this stitch.

Nos. 15, 16 AND 17.—POINT DE SORRENTO OR TWO STITCH.—For this stitch, several button-hole stitches are worked close together, and are made in each line as belonging to each other; they are not separated by any stitch. No. 17 represents this stitch as worked for an edge; this, as well as the two stitch (No. 15), makes a very firm edge ornament. No. 16 gives a single-dotted pattern of two button-hole stitches for filling in odd-shaped spaces.

Nos. 18 AND 20.—VENETIAN BARS.—The bar at No. 18 is so simple that it really needs no description. It is worked over two straight threads in reverse button-hole stitch. No. 20 shows the Venetian bar used as the veining of a leaf and worked upon Sorrento bars.

No. 19.—TREBLE LOOP STITCH.—This is a variety of the Point de Bruxelles stitch; three single stitches being worked in the large loop. The effect is very open and lace-like.

Nos. 21, 22 AND 23.—POINT DE SORRENTO.—These stitches represent the three stitch, two and four stitch and one and three stitch respectively. They are varied patterns of the plain button-hole stitch worked in groups of the number given and are readily accomplished by glancing at the engraving.

Nos. 24, 25 AND 26.—POINT DE VENISE OR SIDE STITCH: BUTTON-HOLE STITCH BACKWARDS.—This effective button-hole looping consists of, first, a common button-hole stitch, as a kind of footing, and then a second looped into it. No. 24 shows, in large size, the mode of working very beautiful point de Venise, either for an outer edge or for patterns, by looping three or four stitches into the first large button-hole stitch, which makes a thick scollop. The stitch is worked from left to right, like Brussels point. Work 1 loose button-hole stitch, and in this stitch work 4 button-hole stitches tightly drawn up, then work another loose button-hole stitch, then 4 more tight button-hole stitches in the loose one; repeat to the end of the row, and fasten off. It is usually called side stitch, as, after making the single net

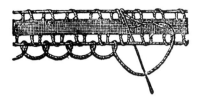

NO. 12.—POINT DE BRUXELLES.
(SINGLE NET STITCH.)

NO. 13.—POINT DE BRUXELLES.
(BRUSSELS POINT)
WORKED IN A SQUARE.

NO. 14.—POINT DE BRUXELLES.
WORKED IN ROWS.

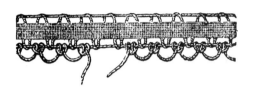

NO. 15.—POINT DE SORRENTO.
(TWO STITCH.)

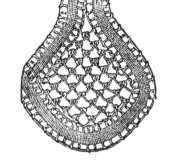

NO. 16.—TWO STITCH WORKED IN ROWS.

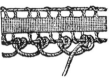

NO. 17.—POINT DE
SORRENTO.
(SECOND METHOD.)

NO. 18.—VENETIAN BARS.

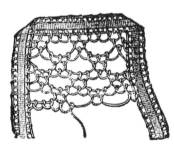

NO. 19.—POINT DE BRUXELLES.
(TREBLE LOOP STITCH.)

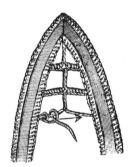

NO. 20.—VENETIAN BARS.

NO. 21.—POINT DE SORRENTO.
(THREE STITCH.)

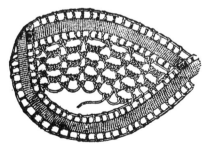

NO. 22.—POINT DE SORRENTO.
(FOUR STITCH.)

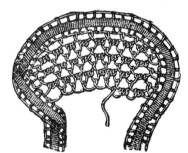

NO. 23.—POINT DE SORRENTO.
(ONE AND THREE STITCH.)

47

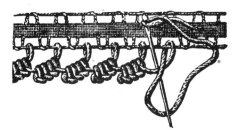

No. 24.—Point de Venise.
(Side Stitch.)

No. 25.—Point de Venise.
(Full Size.)

No. 26.—Point de Venise.
(Worked Loosely.)

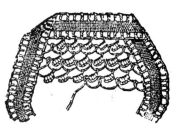

No. 27.—Point de Venise.
(Side and Net Stitch.)

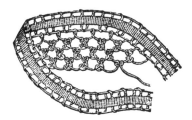

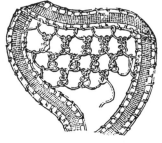

No. 28.—Point de Venise.
(Second Method.)

No. 29.—Point de Venise.
(Third Method.)

No. 30.—Point de Venise.
(Fourth Method.)

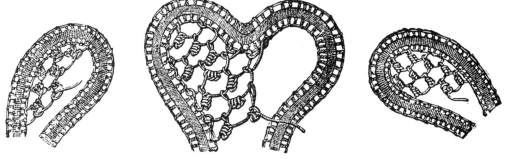

No. 31.

No. 32.

No. 33.

Point de Venise Stitch Employed for Filling In Various Shapes.

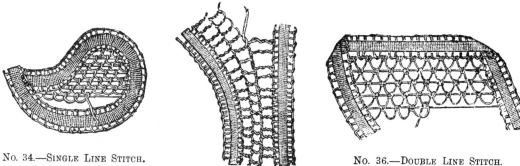

No. 34.—Single Line Stitch.

No. 35.—Point d'Espagne.

No. 36.—Double Line Stitch.

stitch, three or four stitches are worked into the single stitch from the side instead of straight in front as in Nos. 21 and 23. No. 25 gives the edging in the size it would generally appear; No. 26 with the stitches farther apart; consequently the pattern is more open.

Nos. 27, 28, 29, 30, 31, 32 AND 33.—POINT DE VENISE.—These are all varieties of the same stitch. No. 27 represents the Point de Venise stitch with the second row worked back in single net stitch. The three patterns represented in Nos. 28, 29 and 31 are very similar; about two or three button-hole stitches are worked close together, downward, as shown in the design. These serve for enclosing patterns, or they may be arranged in the corded pattern, as the point d'Anvers, for thick patterns. No. 30 gives this stitch worked forward and backward as a pattern, with a line of plain button-hole stitches forming a stripe pattern. No. 32 gives a pattern, with the same thick scollops worked forward and backward, and is very pretty as a guipure ground between thick arabesque patterns. By working downward in the large button-hole scollop, the pattern represented in No. 33 is formed, which is equally pretty worked in single lines, for enclosing large patterns. No. 33 is worked from right to left so as to bring the side stitches, when worked, all running in one direction, and the loops uniform. Worked from left to right it would look entirely different and it would also be impossible to keep the work even.

Nos. 34 AND 36.—SINGLE AND DOUBLE LINE STITCH.—This pretty and effective stitch is easily worked. No 34 gives the single line pattern with button-hole stitches over the thread placed across, and from which many other effective stitches may be made. The stitch should be worked from left to right, so that each worked line is begun at the same side. The single line is drawn across from right to left, and the second and every stitch-row is made taking in the straight thread as seen in the engraving. No. 36 represents the same stitch with two instead of one button-hole stitch in each group.

No. 35.—POINT D'ESPAGNE, OR SPANISH POINT.—This variety of stitch is worked from left to right, as follows: Insert the needle in the edge of the braid, keeping the thread turned to the right, and bringing it out inside the loop formed by the thread (see illustration); the needle must pass from the back of the loop entirely through it. Pass the needle under the stitch and bring it out in front, thus twice twisting the thread, which produces the cord-like appearance of this stitch. At the end of each row fasten to the braid and sew back, inserting the needle once in every open stitch. This illustration shows how the length of the stitch and the number of the twists may be increased to suit the filling-in of an irregular space.

No. 37.—BRUGES STITCH IN SIMPLE FORM.—Many consider the Bruges stitch difficult to make, and though at first glance it may appear intricate, with a little practice there is no reason why this should be considered any more perplexing than any of the other stitches. The Bruges stitches were formerly used only in making Bruges lace, but in the modern laces almost all the different stitches are employed; and in consequence of this and the combination of the different braids some remarkably handsome laces are produced.

On the right hand side of the illustration the Bruges stitch is shown in its simple form, as a filling-in or foundation stitch, which is often used where light bars are needed. It is made in the following manner:

Fasten the thread in the lower right hand side and carry it across to the braid opposite, fasten with a button-hole stitch and overcast the braid one sixteenth of an inch to the left. Work a button-hole stitch over the single thread just made across the work; over this button-hole stitch work three more button-hole stitches close together exactly as was explained for the point de Venise. Two, or preferably three, are used instead of four, as in the point de Venise; the latter is worked much more loosely, the button-hole stitches in the Bruges stitch being drawn very tight to form the little "knots." If this is not done, the work will look loose and unsubstantial and the effect of the knots which is characteristic of the Bruges stitch will be destroyed. It will also be observed that these knots hold the parallel threads in place and give the dainty appearance to the lace when finished.

After the knot is made carry the thread down to the first braid and insert the needle one-sixteenth of an inch from the first thread. Overcast the braid for half an inch, carry the thread across to the opposite braid and fasten with a button-hole stitch; overcast one-sixteenth of an inch and work a knot for the second row exactly like the first.

No. 38.—BRUGES LACE FILLING-IN STITCH.—When the stitch is to be used for filling in a space which is square or nearly so, similar to the lower part of illustration No. 38, the work is done in much the same manner. Fasten the thread in the lower right-hand corner and overcast the edge of the braid for half an inch, carry the thread across to the opposite braid, keeping the line parallel with the braid at the right-hand side and fasten with button-hole stitch: overcast one-sixteenth of an inch to the left. About one-eighth of an inch from the braid work a button-hole stitch over the long, single thread just made across the work; over this button-hole stitch work three other button-hole stitches as explained for the simple Bruges stitch; carry the thread down for half an inch and work another button-hole stitch with three more button-hole stitches over this.

Continue making knots half an inch apart until the end of the long single thread at the starting point of the braid is reached. Overcast the braid for half an inch, carry the thread across to the opposite braid parallel with the first, and fasten with a button-hole stitch. Overcast the braid one-sixteenth of an inch to the left: make the first knot directly on a line with the first knot of the preceding row, and the next knot exactly half an inch from this.

These rows of knots must be kept perfectly parallel, so that when the space is filled in each row of knots will form a perfectly straight line. When the number of lines necessary for filling the space has been completed, turn the work so that the new lines will intersect the first series exactly in the centre between the knots of the finished rows.

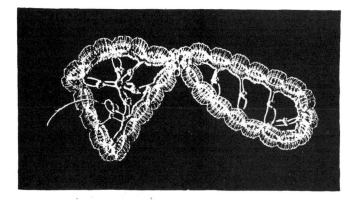

No. 37.—Bruges Stitch in Simple Form.

No. 38.—Bruges Lace Fill-ing-In Stitch.

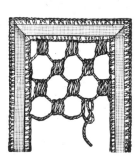

No. 40.—Point de Grecque.
(Square Stitch.)

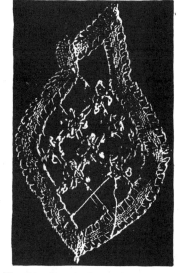

No. 39.—Bruges Stitch in Rosettes.

No. 42.—Cone Stitch in Triangles.

No. 41.—Cone Stitch in Squares.

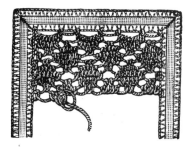

No. 43.—Point de Valenciennes.
(Diamond Stitch.)

No. 44.—Point de Grecque Bars.

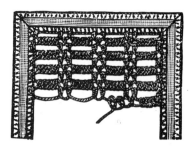

No. 45.—One and Five Stitch.

The work is now in the same position as for the first series of lines. Overcast the braid until a thread carried across from the stopping point to the braid on the opposite side will pass directly through the centre of the space between the knots; insert the needle in the braid—about one thread to the left of the centre, so that the double line and not the first thread alone will be half-way between the knots. Fasten this with a button-hole stitch and overcast the braid one-sixteenth of an inch to the right. After the stitch has been mastered this button-hole stitch for fastening may be omitted, if desired, and the braid simply overcast.

Work a Bruges stitch an eighth of an inch from the braid, carry the thread down and work a button-hole stitch directly at the intersection, by placing the needle under the three threads; then make a spider's web by passing the working thread under and over * as many times as will be found necessary for the space to be filled in. If the space between the knots is very wide, the "spider" will have to be large in proportion, as seen in the yoke illustrated on page 31. Take a stitch over two threads of the spider to stay it; carry the thread down and make a Bruges stitch half-way between the knot just made and the next intersection. After which make a button-hole stitch and spider *at* the intersection. Continue in this way until the space is filled in, keeping the lines and knots perfectly parallel.

No. 39.—BRUGES STITCH IN ROSETTES.—This stitch is made precisely the same as No. 38 until the * is reached; after this point work as follows:

Make the spider for three or four rounds, carry the thread to the first space at the left and work a button-hole stitch by taking up two threads of the spider. In this stitch work three more button-hole stitches as before, working toward the centre. Take a stitch through the centre of the spider's-web, drawing the needle out at the next space and here work another knot.

After the fourth or last knot has been worked take a stitch through the spider and carry the thread down. Work a Bruges stitch on the single thread half-way between the rosette and the next intersection. If the rosettes are desired very close together, these knots may be omitted, as seen in illustration No. 39. Work the next rosette at the next intersection and continue until the space is filled in.

No. 40.—POINT DE GRECQUE OR SQUARE STITCH.—Point de Grecque is made from left to right, and is worked backward and forward. It is begun by one stitch in loose point de Bruxelles and is followed by three of close point d'Espagne; then one Bruxelles, three point d'Espagne, to the end of the row; in returning work in the same manner.

No. 41.—CONE STITCH IN SQUARES.—This stitch is useful as a variation, and resembles the point de reprise of guipure lace-making. It is worked in a similar manner, over and under the sides of squares formed by intersecting straight lines of the thread.

No. 42.—CONE STITCH IN TRIANGLES.—This stitch is worked by darning over and under two threads forming a triangle. The space is filled by parallel and crosswise bars placed at equal distances, and on the triangles thus produced point de reprise is worked.

No. 43.—POINT DE VALENCIENNES, OR DIAMOND STITCH.—This stitch appears complicated, but it is really easy to work. Begin at the left hand and work point de Bruxelles stitches at unequal distances, every alternate stitch being the larger.

Second row.—Upon the first large or long stitch work 9 close button-hole stitches, then 1 short point de Bruxelles stitch under the one above, then 9 close stitches, and so on to the end of the row.

Third row.—Make 5 close button-hole stitches in the 9 of previous row, 1 short point de Bruxelles, 2 close (in the Bruxelles stitch), 1 short point de Bruxelles, 5 close, 1 short point de Bruxelles, 2 close, 1 short, 5 close, 1 short and repeat.

Fourth row.—Make 5 close, 1 short point de Bruxelles, 2 close, 1 short, 5 close, 1 short, 2 close, 1 short and repeat. Continue the rows until sufficient of the pattern is worked.

No. 44.—POINT DE GRECQUE BARS.—These bars are so simply made that they are great favorites with beginners. They are begun at the top of the point, one straight thread being carried to the bottom; then the cross bars are worked after the method seen in the illustration.

No. 45.—ONE AND FIVE STITCH.—This stitch is worked as follows, from left to right:

First row.—Make 1 long, loose stitch in point de Bruxelles, and 1 short, loose one alternately to end of row.

Second row.—Make 7 tight point de Bruxelles in the one long, loose stitch, and 2 short, loose point de Bruxelles in the short, loose stitch on previous row, and repeat across the row.

Third row.—Same as first.

Nos. 46, 47, 48, 49 AND 51.—POINT D'ANVERS OR CORDED BUTTON-HOLE STITCH.—These are all varieties of the same stitch. The first row is worked with button-hole stitches. In returning, in this pattern, the thread is twisted through the button-hole stitch and is enclosed by the fresh button-hole stitches. This variation is a near approach to the point de Malines. The button-hole stitch is worked between the cording-stitch. Nos. 47 and 49 show leaves in point de Bruxelles and pointd'Anvers, and are worked in button-hole stitch, with and without the thread being drawn through; and, in No. 49, filled up as shown, by cross-stitch. Nos. 48 and 51 give the variations of these patterns, as seen in the large and small patterns of Antwerp lace, and known to very many ladies as point d'Anvers. No. 48 belongs to the order of button-hole stitches, all the patterns of which being worked by drawing the thread through, may be classed among the Antwerp stitches (point d'Anvers).

It need scarcely be mentioned that the long threads between the spaces are wound round **with**

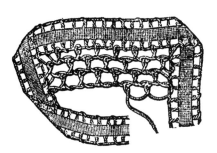

No. 46.—CORDED BUTTON-HOLE STITCH.

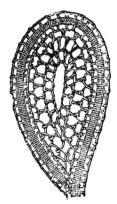

No. 47.—POINT D'ANVERS OR
CORDED BUTTON-HOLE STITCH.
(SECOND METHOD.)

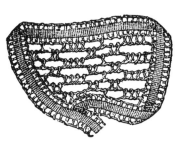

No. 48.—CORDED BUTTON-HOLE
STITCH. (THIRD METHOD.)

No. 49.—CORDED BUTTON-HOLE
STITCH. (FOURTH METHOD.)

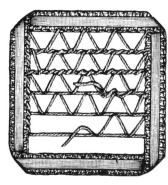

No. 50.—CORDED GROUNDWORK
STITCH.

No. 51.—CORDED BUTTON-HOLE STITCH.
(FIFTH METHOD.)

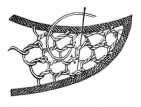

No. 52.—POINT DE TULLE.

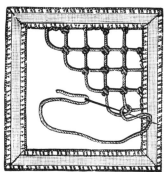

No. 53.—POINT DE FILLET (NET
GROUNDWORK STITCH).

No. 54.—NET GROUNDWORK WITH EM-
BROIDERED SQUARES.

No. 55.—POINT TURQUE.
(SECOND METHOD.)

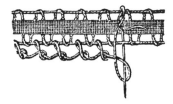

No. 56.—POINT TURQUE.
(TURKISH STITCH.)

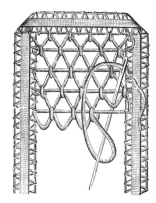

No. 57.—TURQUE AND LINE STITCH.

52

several stitches. No 46 is a slight variety of the same stitch seen at No. 95 on page 60 under the name of Italian Lace Stitch.

No. 50.—CORDED GROUNDWORK STITCH.—At Nos. 1 and 2 a description of the method of making Sorrento bars is given, while at No. 9 is a description of the Twisted Russian stitch. The two methods are combined in the work seen at No. 50, where the process is so clearly illustrated that a mere novice in lace-work could not fail to produce it perfectly. The combined stitch is used in filling in squares, triangles, etc., etc.

No. 52.—POINT DE TULLE.—This stitch is used as a ground-work for very fine work, and is worked in rows backward and forward in the same stitch as open point d'Espagne. When this is completed the work is gone over a second time by inserting the needle under one twisted bar, bringing it out and insert-it at + and bringing it out again at the dot. This produces a close double twist that is very effective.

No. 53.—POINT DE FILLET OR NET GROUNDWORK STITCH.—This stitch is also represented at No. 54, but the method of making the knot is here very clearly illustrated. It is used for groundwork where Brussels net is not imitated, and is very effective wherever it is used It is begun in the corner or cross-wise of the space to be filled. A loose point de Bruxelles stitch is first taken and fastened to the braid, then passed twice through the braid, as shown in the illustration, and worked in rows backward and forward, as follows: 1 point de Bruxelles stitch, then before proceeding to the next stitch, pass the needle *under* the knot, *over* the thread, and again *under* it, as shown in the illustration. This stitch is very quickly worked.

No. 54.—NET GROUNDWORK WITH EMBROIDERED SQUARES.—The network seen in this engraving is the first stitch mentioned, while the block-work is the second. Both are clearly illustrated and need no written explanation of the method employed in making them.

Nos. 55, 56 AND 57.—POINT TURQUE OR TURKISH POINT.—This easy and effective stitch is very appropriate for filling either large or small spaces: the thread employed should be varied in thickness according to the size of the space to be filled. No. 55 is worked similarly to No. 36, the difference being in the line which is clearly shown in the engraving.

First row. (see No. 57).—Work a loop in the braid, bringing the thread from right to left, passing the needle through the twist and through the loop (see engraving); draw up tight and repeat.

Second row.—1 straight thread from right to left.

Third row.—Work the same as first, using the straight thread instead of the braid, and passing the needle through the loop of the previous row, as shown in the illustration. No. 56 represents the stitch on one line, which would make a very pretty outer edge. No. 55 represents the dotted pattern, consisting of one plain and one looped button-hole stitch. which is a pretty variation of No. 56, and might also be worked over threads placed across.

No. 58.—POINT D'ANVERS BAR.—Two upright bars form the foundation. The thread is carried over and under them as seen in the engraving, the side loops being added by the method depicted at the top of the point. The over and under work in point d'Anvers bars, without the side loops, is often used for plain bars for filling in odd places or wheels in heavy lace.

Nos. 59, 61 AND 64.—LIMOGES LACE STITCH.—The peculiarity of Limoges lace consists in its being made with plain braid; and the edge is all worked to it. The braid is shown very greatly increased in size in the engravings, which also show the proper mode of working the lace.

In working Limoges lace it is very important that the braid be soft and well made, and that the thread be of a suitable size and quality. In black (silk) materials it is equally as beautiful as in white, and better adapted for some purposes.

Tack the braid upon the design, holding it rather loosely, as the semi-transparency thus secured adds much to the beauty of the lace. Then run a very fine cotton through the whole length of the braid, carefully keeping it *inside* the curves, crossing from one edge of the braid to the other wherever the pattern demands it. The curves will then retain their correct shape when taken off the paper. When arriving at a corner where the braid folds over, a few extra stitches will be required to make it neat and firm. Then commence the edge, which consists only of a loose button-hole stitch, with a tight one of the same kind in every loose one, so that the edge is entirely finished in one row. When edging the braid nearest that already done, the bars must be introduced to connect them. This edge, with the bars is also done in one row. When the braids so nearly touch as to leave no room for a bar, they should be joined by a herring-bone stitch.

When the space is so large that it must be filled up with a net-work of bars, instead of passing the needle through an opposite stitch, pass it round the middle of a neighboring bar, making a tight button-hole stitch upon the perfect bar to secure the one in progress in its proper place. Several bars may be made, when desired, by taking the single thread from bar to bar, or stitch to stitch, working the twisting round the already half-made bars as you return. The extra edge seen is only the same stitch as the ordinary edge, worked with three tight stitches instead of one. The little spot seen in several places is made thus: Make one bar across the space, and complete the second one (which crosses it) as far as the centre, where the two bars cross each other; next darn round, under one thread and over another, until the spot is large enough, then finish the twisting round of the imperfect bar.

No. 60.—SPINNING-WHEEL ROSETTE.—These rosettes are very useful for filling the empty spaces in foundations of patterns. The engraving gives a wheel in which the thread is twisted over six thread bars in a line (point de Venise).

53

NO. 58.—POINT D'ANVERS BAR.

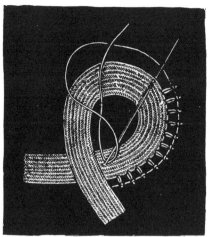

NO. 59.—LIMOGES LACE STITCH.
(FIRST MOVEMENT.)

NO. 60.—SPINNING-WHEEL ROSETTE.

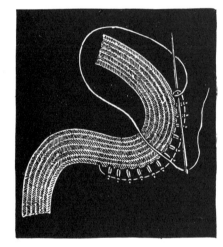

NO. 61.—LIMOGES LACE STITCH.
(SECOND MOVEMENT.)

NO. 62. — QUARTERFOIL
IN BULLION STITCH.

NO. 63. WHEEL WITH
PICOTS.

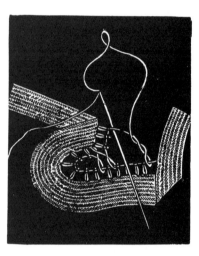

NO. 64.—LIMOGES LACE STITCH.
(THIRD MOVEMENT.)

NO. 65.—D'ALENÇON BARS.

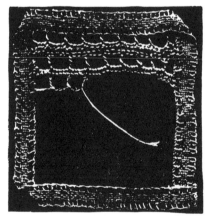

NO. 66.—CHURCH LACE STITCH.

NO. 67.—PLAIN VENETIAN BARS.

54

Nos. 62 AND 63.—PICOTS.—No. 62 shows a very effective picot, which may be worked round the threads that cross each other or round a little spinning-stitch or wheel; it may also be used for flowers. For this kind of picot make first a button-hole stitch round the netted cross, push the needle in it, and wind the cotton ten or twelve times round for one picot; then carefully draw another button-hole stitch round the netted cross to fasten the finished picot and to prepare for the next. No. 63 represents a finished wheel surrounded with very pretty picots.

No. 65.—D'ALENÇON BARS.—These bars are worked upon point de Bruxelles edging, and are only applied to the inner part of a pattern, never being used as ground-work bars. The thread is merely passed three times over and under the point de Bruxelles stitches, the length of these bars being regulated by the space to be filled ; when the third bar is completed a tight point de Bruxelles stitch fastens off the bars, and the thread is passed through the next point de Bruxelles stitch.

No. 66.—CHURCH STITCH.—This stitch is used alone for church lace. It is very simple, consisting only of button-hole stitches arranged as follows : Make the first row of stitches as seen in No. 12. Then work a close row of button-hole stitches (as seen in the second row of No. 66); work back another row, but instead of taking the stitch *between* two stitches of the first row, take it through the *twist or loop* of a stitch. Work the third row in the same manner. Then repeat the first row of twisted loops and repeat also the three rows of button-hole stitches. The engraving shows the development of the work but is not a design. The twisted row and the three solid rows alternate in all designs.

No. 67.—PLAIN VENETIAN BARS.—These bars are worked so as to form squares, triangles, etc., in button-hole stitch upon a straight thread.

The *arrow* in the illustration points to the direction for working the next stitch.

No. 68.—BUTTON-HOLE BAR WITH LACE PICOT.—This stitch is composed of a bar, the foundation threads of which are carried from one space to another and back, several times, according to the number of the thread and the thickness of the bar required. These bars are wrought over with button-hole stitches and picots. If the bar is short, one picot is placed in the centre; if longer, several picots may be arranged at intervals.

Picots are of several forms and worked in as many different ways, the one illustrated at figure No. 68 being worked in the following manner : The foundation bars are laid as explained, and five or six button-hole stitches are worked; the thread is then passed over the foundation threads without the button-hole stitch. Fasten the loop with a pin as seen in illustration, then slip the needle horizontally under the three threads and draw the knot up tight, close to the last button-hole stitch. This picot is often called purl picot and may be given a slightly heavier look by having two or three instead of one fastening stitch.

No. 69.—BAR WITH POINT DE VENISE PICOT.—This picot is started the same as that shown at No. 68. With the pin holding the loop in position, place the needle under these stitches but over the thread (see illustration); over these work four or five tight point de Bruxelles stitches, starting close to the pin and covering the entire bar. Insert the pin in the loop distant from the bar the width of the number of stitches intended to be worked over it.

No. 70.—PICOT IN BULLION STITCH.—Lay the foundation threads as explained and over these threads work six tight button-hole stitches; if but one picot is to be worked, half the bar must be covered with button-hole stitches, next work one button-hole stitch, a little looser, pass the needle between these stitches and wind the thread eight or nine times round the point. The coils must be drawn up close, without lapping, so that the needle may be drawn through easily.

Place the thumb of the left hand upon the coil and draw the needle through gently. If this is thrust through rather far before beginning to wind the coils, it will be found easier to pull it through. The larger the picot desired the greater number of coils necessary.

Continue to work button-hole stitches covering the remainder of the bar. This is a quick mode of making the picot and imitates most closely real Spanish lace.

Nos. 71 AND 72.—RALEIGH BARS.—These bars are much used in making Battenberg lace and are very effective. They are worked over a foundation or network of coarse thread, and are twisted in places so that they will more easily fall into the desired form.

By following the numbering from 1 to 21 in No. 72 a square place may be easily filled, and portions of this arrangement applied to form groundwork of any shape desired. Upon this groundwork tight point de Bruxelles stitches are made, and the dot is worked upon these in any one of the ways illustrated and explained for Nos. 68, 69, 70 and 73. Illustration No. 71 shows the finished Raleigh bars.

Illustration No. 75 also shows how this stitch may be applied as a *regular* groundwork, but the beauty of old point groundwork bars consists in variety of form.

No. 73.—BAR WITH BUTTON-HOLE PICOT.—Here the bar is more than half covered with button-hole stitches. Insert the needle in the fourth or fifth stitch from the last, and back and forth until there are three threads, cover these with point de Bruxelles stitches forming a semi-circle. Continue covering the bar as in the beginning. These picots are often used for a scollop around the edge of the lace.

No. 74.—DOTTED POINT DE VENISE BARS.—These bars are very pretty and are worked as explained for No. 69. Five button-hole stitches are worked over the bar, but instead of four or five stitches, simply three tight point de Bruxelles stitches are used to form the picot.

55

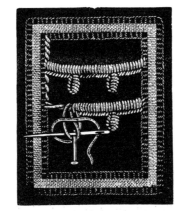

NO. 68.—BUTTON-HOLE BAR WITH LACE PICOT.

NO. 69.—BAR WITH POINT DE VENISE PICOT.

NO. 70.—PICOT IN BULLION STITCH.

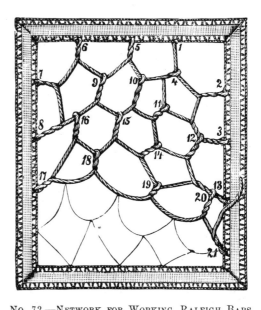

NO. 71.—RALEIGH BARS.

NO. 72.—NETWORK FOR WORKING RALEIGH BARS.

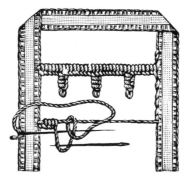

NO. 73.—BAR WITH BUTTON-HOLE PICOT.

NO. 74.—DOTTED POINT DE VENISE BARS.

NO. 75.—BULLION PICOTS WORKED IN SQUARES.

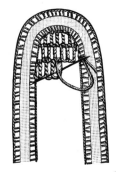

No. 76—Single Point d'Es-
pagne.

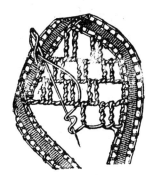

No. 77.—Double Point d'Espagne.

No. 78.—Treble Point d'Espagne.

No. 79.—Point d'Espagne.
(Six Stitch.)

No. 80.—Point d'Espagne.
(Two and Six Stitch.)

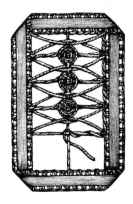

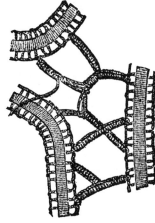

No. 81.—Point d'Angleterre Rosettes.

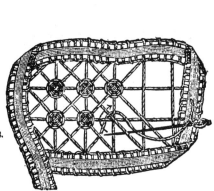

No. 83.—d'Angleterre Rosettes.
(Lattice Pattern.)

No. 82.—Bars of Point d'Angleterre.

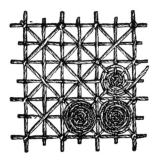

No. 84.—Plain Wheels on
Lattice-Work.

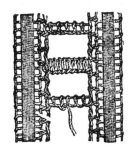

No. 85.—Venetian Button-Hole
Bars.

No 86—Button-Hole Stitch Bars.

The making of the dots or purls mentioned as picots is an important feature in bar work. All three names are employed for the same class of stitch.

No. 75.—BULLION PICOTS WORKED IN SQUARES.—This method is fully described in connection with the making of the Raleigh bars seen at Nos. 71 and 72, and requires no description at this point. All dots and picots render work much more effective, and may be introduced at will by the worker.

The word "Bar" is applied to the many stitches used to connect the various parts of lace, and the beauty of the work depends greatly upon the class of bar selected and its suitability to the lace stitches used.

Nos. 76, 77, 78, 79 AND 80.—POINT D'ESPAGNE OR SPANISH POINT.—This variety of stitch is worked from left to right as follows: Insert the needle in the edge of the braid, keeping the thread turned to the right, and bringing it out inside the loop formed by the thread (see illustration); the needle must pass from the back of the loop entirely through it. Pass the needle under the stitch and bring it out in front, thus twice twisting the thread, which produces the cord-like appearance of this stitch. At the end of each row fasten to the braid and sew back, inserting the needle once in every open stitch. No. 78 is worked in exactly the same way as the stitch just mentioned, as follows : 3 close stitches, 1 open, 3 close to the end of each row. Sew back, and in the next row make 1 open, 3 close, 1 open, 3 close to the end ; repeat the rows as far as necessary, taking care that the close and open stitches follow in regular order. Diamonds, stars, squares, blocks and various other pretty patterns may be formed by this stitch.

No. 81.—POINT D'ANGLETERRE ROSETTES.—This design is worked as follows : Cover the space to be filled in with lines of thread about an eighth of an inch apart; then form cross-lines, intersecting those already made and passing alternately under and over them ; work a rosette on every spot where two lines cross by working over and under the two lines about 16 times round ; then twist the threads twice round the groundwork thread, and begin to form another rosette at the crossing threads.

Wheels and rosettes are used to fill up spaces, or in combination, to form lace.

No. 82.—BARS OF POINT D'ANGLETERRE.—These bars may be worked singly or to fill up a space, as in the illustration. Work rosettes as in point d'Angleterre ; when each rosette is finished twist the thread up the foundation thread to the top, fasten with one stitch, then pass it under the parallel line running through the centre and over into the opposite braid ; repeat on each side of each rosette, inserting the threads as seen in the illustration.

No. 83.—POINT D'ANGLETERRE: ROSETTE PATTERN.—There are several kinds of rosette patterns, which, according to the number of threads stretched across, require a looser or closer spinning-stitch for the wheels. The spaces must be most regularly and evenly arranged. For the rosette in No. 81 the threads must be first of all stretched in one direction, then plaited through in the opposite direction ; they are then worked in lines, according to design. The rosettes in the double trellis pattern, No. 83 have at first only one of the diagonal threads stretched across ; the second slanting thread is placed in the working of the wheels as shown in the illustration. This is employed for filling-in large spaces. Rosettes with loose thread-squares, represented in the bars at No. 82, are particularly intended for leaves; although they may be adapted to spaces of various shapes.

No. 84.—PLAIN WHEELS ON LATTICE-WORK.—These wheels may be used in open spaces and may be very easily made from the engraving. They are much like the wheels used in drawn-work—indeed many of the stitches used in lace are identical with those used in drawn-work.

No. 85.—VENETIAN BUTTON-HOLE BARS.—In working these bars there is always at least three, if not five, threads stretched across and worked over very closely with the button-hole stitch (Point d'esprit); in working these, the cross-bars branch off from the principal bars, and may be ornamented with picots.

No. 86.—BUTTON-HOLE STITCH BAR.—Stretch the thread across and work it over like the Sorrento bar, returning with a few button-hole stitches, and then wind the thread again through as seen in the illustration.

Nos. 87 AND 89.—FLAT SPIDER OR WHEEL.—In making a flat spider or wheel an uneven number of bars or spokes should be provided for the foundation in order to bring the weaving over and under out evenly. When the bars are even in number the work will not finish properly or after the manner intended. The engravings show a finished flat spider and the detail of making.

No. 88.—LEAF ORNAMENTATION.—This consists of a row of point d'Espagne, enclosed by a very thick stripe of point de Bruxelles, with always four button-hole stitches in one point d'Espagne stitch. A line of point de Venise in thick scollops forms the inner edge.

Nos. 90 AND 91.—LEAF STITCH.—This stitch is worked similar to No. 44. The thread extends from bottom to top and the veins are laid in as seen in the illustration. These veins are darned under and over the foundation threads.

No. 92.—POINT DE VENISE BARS (EDGED).—Begin at the right hand and stretch a line of thread to the left side of the braid, fastening it with one tight stitch of point de Bruxelles. Upon this line work a succession of tight point de Bruxelles stitches. Then in every third stitch work one point de Venise stitch.

No. 93.—ROSETTE IN RAISED POINT D'ANGLETERRE.—This rosette is worked in a manner similar to the plain spider-web, the difference being that after each stitch is passed round and under the bars, the thread is passed loosely around in the reverse direction, as shown in the illustration, before proceeding to make the next stitch. But in making this rosette with the wrong side up, the thread must be passed round every bar, which gives the raised bars on the right side when the work is finished.

NO. 87.—FLAT SPIDER OR SORRENTO WHEEL.

NO. 88.—LEAF ORNAMENTATION.

NO. 89.—DETAIL OF FLAT SPIDER OR SORRENTO WHEEL.

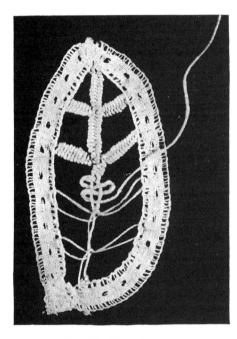

NO. 90.—LEAF STITCH.

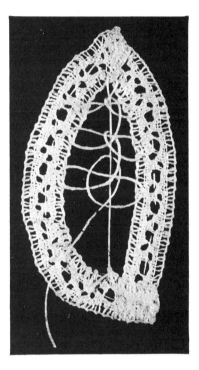

NO. 91.—DETAIL OF LEAF STITCH.

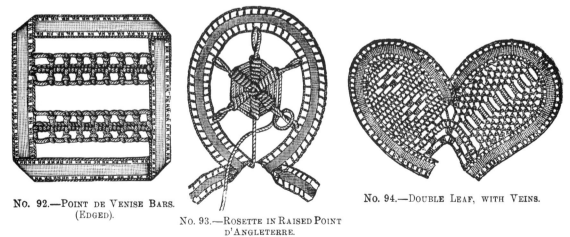

NO. 92.—POINT DE VENISE BARS. (EDGED).

NO. 93.—ROSETTE IN RAISED POINT D'ANGLETERRE.

NO. 94.—DOUBLE LEAF, WITH VEINS.

59

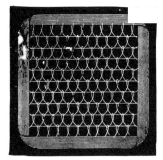

No. 95.—Italian Lace Stitch.

No. 96.—Trefoil with Various Stitches.

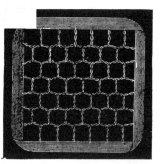

No. 97.—Italian Ground Stitch.

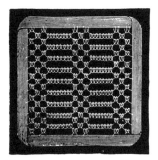

No. 98.—Flemish Lace Stitch.

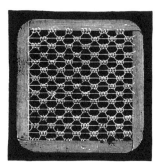

No. 99.—Cobweb Lace Stitch.

No. 101.—Genoa Lace Stitch.

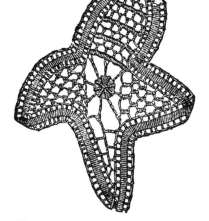

No. 100.—Rose Point Lace Stitch.

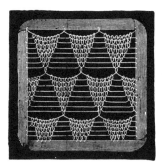

No. 102.—Fan Lace Stitch.

No. 103.—Spanish Net Stitch.

No. 104.—Trefoil with Various Stitches.

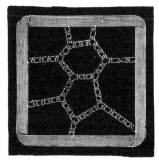

No. 105.—Open Lace Bars.

60

No. 94.—DOUBLE LEAF WITH VEINS.—The pattern of the leaf on the left is in point d'Espagne; that on the right is in loose point de Bruxelles, and has a vein. Such patterns, without reference to the kind of stitches are called point de Valenciennes.

No. 95.—ITALIAN LACE STITCH (ALSO CALLED POINT D'ANVERS.—Commence at the right side and pass the thread to the left.

First row.—Make a loose button-hole stitch in the braid to form a loop, then pass the needle under the line of thread, making the loops an eighth of an inch apart.

Second row.—Pass the thread back to the left, make a button-hole stitch in every loop, and pass the needle under the line of thread, after each button-hole stitch.

Nos. 96 AND 104.—TREFOILS WITH VARIOUS STITCHES.—These are only guides to show how the separate divisions of large leaves may be filled up with various lace stitches, and joined together in the middle with a wheel, star, etc. Such stars or wheels may be worked in any of the various lace stitches of the designs already explained.

No. 97.—ITALIAN GROUND STITCH.—Commence at the left side, and work as follows:

First row.—Make a loose button-hole stitch to form a loop a quarter of an inch wide, and then make a plain stitch into the loop to twist it, and continue to the end.

Second row.—Make two plain stitches into each loop, working back to the left.

Third row.—Repeat first row.

No. 98.—FLEMISH LACE STITCH.—Commence at the right side, and work as follows:

First row.—Work two button-hole stitches close together, miss the space of 2, work 2, miss the space of 8; this will leave a large loop and a small one alternately.

Second row.—Make 8 button-hole stitches in the larger loops, and 2 in the small ones.

Third row.—Repeat the first row, making 2 stitches in each loop of the second row.

No. 99.—COBWEB LACE STITCH.—Commence at the right side, pass the thread to the left, work three button-hole stitches, miss the space of 3, which will leave a small loop, and continue these details to the end.

Second row.—Pass the thread back to the left side, work 3 button-hole stitches in each loop, taking up the line of thread with the loop, as seen in the engravings.

No. 100.—ROSE POINT LACE STITCH.—Make a foundation of single threads, crossing them to form the large squares. Work a button-hole stitch at each crossing to make it firm. Now begin at the top, at the right side and fill the first square with Brussels-net stitches, finishing at the lower left corner. Fill every alternate square in the same way, as seen in the picture.

Now cross the open squares diagonally with two threads, twisting each thread around the adjoining one, as represented. (Carry one thread across all the squares from corner to corner first, then twist back, fastening at the corner started from; cross these threads in the same way from the opposite direction.) When twisting the thread back from the last set of crossings, make a rosette at each centre crossing as follows: Keep the space open with a pin and trace around it with a darning movement five or six times; commence at the single thread and work a close button-hole stitch over the tracing entirely around, and then twist along the single thread to the centre of the next square. This is a very effective design for spaces.

No. 101.—GENOA LACE STITCH.—Commence at the right side, and work as follows:

First row.—Work 4 button-hole stitches, miss the space of 3, work 3, miss the space of 3, work 4. Continue to the end.

Second row.—Work 9 stitches close together, three into the spaces of the 4, and 3 more into the loop at each side of it. Miss the 3 stiches, and make 9 as before.

Third row.—Make 9 close stitches, 3 into the last 3 spaces of the 9, 3 into the loop, and 3 into the first spaces of the next 9, and so on to the end.

Fourth row.—Repeat the first, making the 3 stitches into the loop, and the 4 into the centre spaces of the 9.

No. 102.—FAN LACE STITCH.—Commence at the right side and work as follows:

First row.—Make 1 button-hole stitch and miss the space of 8, which will leave a long loop.

Second row.—Make 8 button-hole stitches in each loop.

Third row.—Make 7 stitches into the spaces between the 8, and so decrease one in every row until only one remains, as may be seen by referring to the illustration.

No. 103.—SPANISH NET STITCH.—The principle of this stitch is the same as that of the Turkish stitch seen at No. 57; it is made with bars and button-hole stitches, and the loose bars are caught to the clusters of three with *two* button-hole stitches.

No. 105—OPEN LACE BARS.—Pass a thread from right to left. Make it firm by working a second stitch into the braid; work two button-hole stitches on this line of thread, close together. Then work 1 button-hole stitch on the lower thread at the left hand side, and draw it close to the 2 stitches on the line of thread. Miss the space of two and repeat.

STITCHES FOR FILLING IN VARIOUS SHAPES, SQUARES, OVALS, ROSETTES. ETC., ETC.

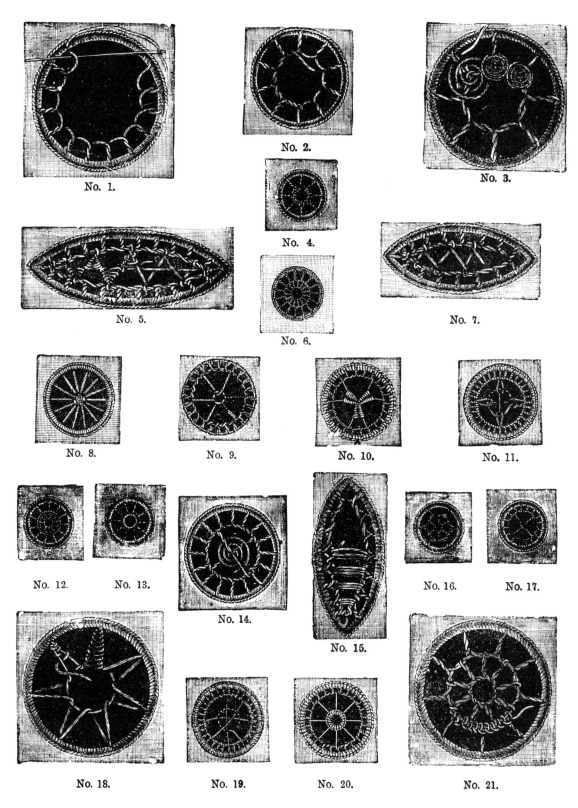

No. 1.

No. 2.

No. 3.

No. 4.

No. 5.

No. 6.

No. 7.

No. 8.

No. 9.

No. 10.

No. 11.

No. 12.

No. 13.

No. 14.

No. 15.

No. 16.

No. 17.

No. 18.

No. 19.

No. 20.

No. 21.

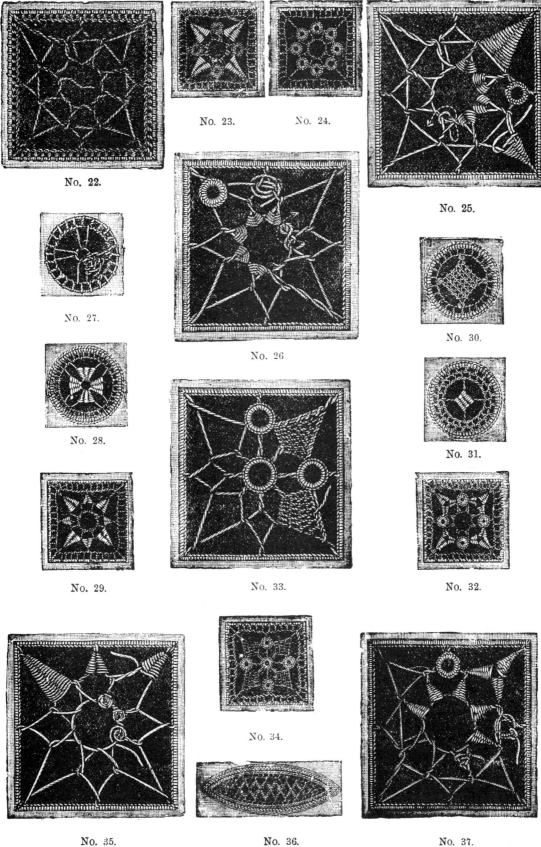

No. 22.

No. 23.

No. 24.

No. 25.

No. 27.

No. 26

No. 30.

No. 28.

No. 31.

No. 29.

No. 33.

No. 32.

No. 35.

No. 34.

No. 36.

No. 37.

STITCHES FOR FILLING IN ROSETTES, OVALS AND SQUARES.

The stitches here shown may be adapted to spaces of various shapes notwithstanding the number of figures illustrated give many varieties for filling in. After the fundamental stitches of the previous chapter have been mastered the forms will be readily worked from different details in increased size, which plan if carefully studied, will be found to be much easier than working from directions.

No. 1.—The great number of these stitches are formed by a row of point de Bruxelles or button-hole stitches worked into the braid which forms the circle or square. This illustration shows the working of this edge. Upon this inner edge the lace stitches are again carried on; in every case, however, the thread is at last looped on the first single bar, and is wound back to the edge, where it is fastened.

No. 2 shows the twisted stitch through the previous row.

No. 3.—The next movement is here plainly pictured so that the mode of working the spinning-wheels over the foundation of corded button-hole bars is very apparent, and will be found very easy to work.

No. 4 —This wheel is similar to No. 3, having tiny spiders close to the centre.

Nos. 5 and 7.—Pyramid or Cone Ovals.—These are worked in cone stitch illustrated at No. 42 page 50. No. 7 shows the detail.

No. 6.—This is worked like No. 2, then a second row of twisted button-hole stitches with a line forming the centre.

Nos. 8 to 13 and 16, 17, 19 and 20.—Wheels with Thread Bars.—A single thread is stretched across, and the work is carried on over the opening, and by cording along the edge. No. 19 shows the mode of stretching the threads across. After having stretched the third thread across, which gives six thread bars, carry the last thread only as far as the middle, and there bend out the cross threads, and draw them round once or twice more with the working thread in order to be able to work a firm open ring in point d'esprit, as shown at No. 20. The thread that is wanting is supplied at the last. No. 8 is a wheel with a thick, round pattern in the centre and has fourteen single thread bars; the raised round in the centre may be either in chain-stitch or a little woven wheel.

No. 14.—Spinning Stitch or Wheel.—These are made by drawing the thread round the lengthened middle points of the stretched threads. The mode of weaving in the thread is clearly shown.

No. 15.—This oval shows the foundation stitches laid and the treble bars across, partly worked.

No. 18.—Pyramid Rosette.—The loose bars are laid and the circle formed, after which the pyramid or cone stitch is darned as for No. 5.

No. 21.—This illustration pictures a treble rosette (twisted button-hole stitch), with the ring filled up. Work two lines of the bars according to previous directions, and then work button-hole stitches round the middle edge.

Nos. 22, 23 and 25.—Squares, with Pyramid Scollops, Point d'Esprit Rings and Patterns of Cross-Stitch.—The threads are stretched across according to No. 22, and then worked according to No. 25, with the same is worked a thick pattern of eight or twelve cross-stitches, lying over each other in each of the little middle triangles, as shown graduated at No. 25. The thread must be laid on afresh for the outer edge, and then a pyramid and a ring worked alternately.

Nos. 24 and 26.—Squares, with Rings in Point d'Esprit, and Patterns of Cross Stitch.—The stretched thread must be fastened with the thread drawn through, without the first loop row shown in No. 22; the second inner row is stretched across, and worked inside, with thick patterns of cross-stitches. At the outer edge are rings in point d'esprit, which join the working thread. These rings extend from one to the other, forming a circle.

Nos. 27 and 28.—Cross Rosette.—After the stretched thread bows are united by a thread ring, the helping cross in the middle must be taken away, and the rosette completed with darning and thick cross stitches.

Nos. 29 and 35.—Squares with Pyramid Scollops and Interwoven Wheels.—The threads are stretched across as before described, and the wheels are interwoven into the inner triangle (No. 35) The outer edge consists of large and small pyramids interwoven, as shown in the design.

No. 30.—Rosette with Square, Fastened with Button-Hole Stitch.—The outline of the square is worked with four button-hole stitches in the open edge, and this is filled up with point d'Anvers, in which the square is again corded all round, and ornamented in the corners with little thick rounds.

No. 31.—Rosette Square.—For this, two bows are required, which are corded and then joined with close cross-stitches, in the form of a little square.

No. 32.—This rosette is worked similar to No. 23, except that three cones form each corner.

Nos. 33 and 34.—Squares with Rings in Point d'Esprit and Open Scollops.—The stretching of the thread differs from No. 22 in the second row, in adding which the inner space is narrowed off to a ring, which is closely worked in point d'esprit, uniting eight radii, forming a star.

As shown in design, the outer edge consists of alternately point d'Espagne scollops and rings in point d'esprit. These may be easily worked from No 33 and must be corded with the thread after they are looped on, so that the next ring may be joined on immediately.

No. 36.—This oval is filled in with double Russian stitch with the bars button-hole stitched.

No. 37.—Square, with Pyramid Scollops and Point d'Esprit Rings.—For this two single loop-lines, with the thread drawn once through for a firm edge, must be worked into each other, exactly according to No. 22, and then according to No. 25, the middle triangles are filled up with single, and the large corner openings with three pyramid scollops. In the four spaces of the outer edge between the corners adjoining the corner pattern, the rings are worked in point d'esprit.

BRAIDS USED IN MODERN LACE-MAKING.

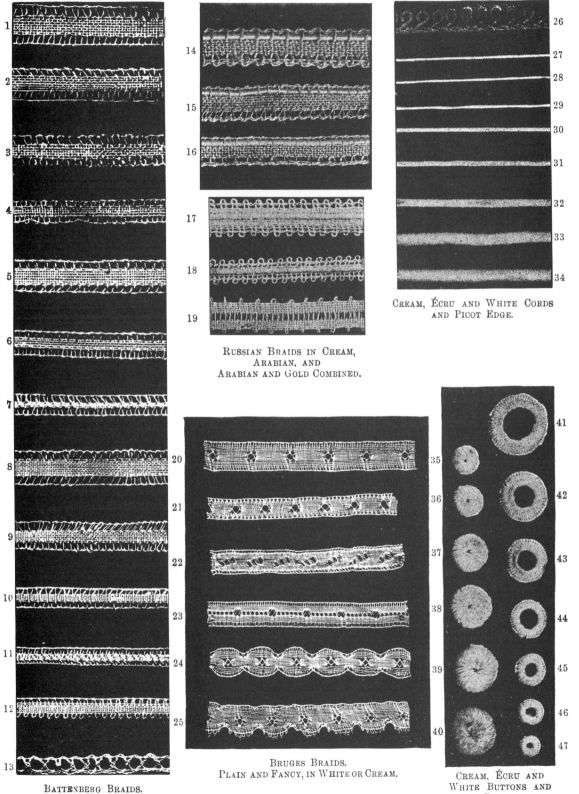

BATTENBERG BRAIDS.

RUSSIAN BRAIDS IN CREAM,
ARABIAN, AND
ARABIAN AND GOLD COMBINED.

CREAM, ÉCRU AND WHITE CORDS
AND PICOT EDGE.

BRUGES BRAIDS.
PLAIN AND FANCY, IN WHITE OR CREAM.

CREAM, ÉCRU AND
WHITE BUTTONS AND
RINGS.

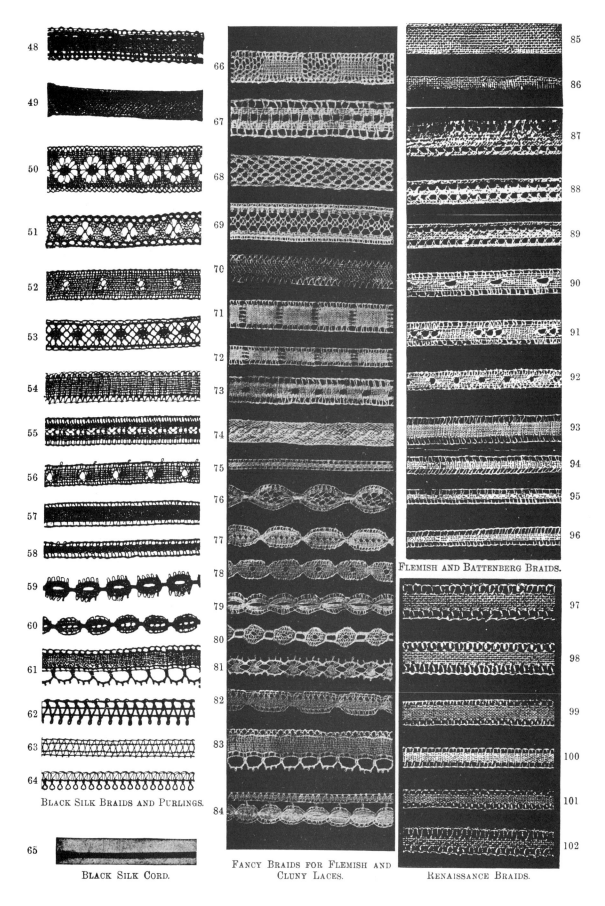

48

49

50

51

52

53

54

55

56

57

58

59

60

61

62

63

64

BLACK SILK BRAIDS AND PURLINGS.

65

BLACK SILK CORD.

66

67

68

69

70

71

72

73

74

75

76

77

78

79

80

81

82

83

84

FANCY BRAIDS FOR FLEMISH AND
CLUNY LACES.

85

86

87

88

89

90

91

92

93

94

95

96

FLEMISH AND BATTENBERG BRAIDS.

97

98

99

100

101

102

RENAISSANCE BRAIDS.

66

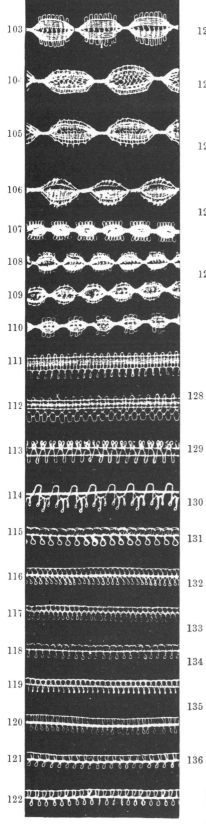

103
10-
105
106
107
108
109
110
111
112
113
114
115
116
117
118
119
120
121
122

HONITON BRAIDS AND PURLINGS.

123
124
125
126
127

HONITON BRAIDS.

128
129
130
131
132
133
134
135
136

CREAM AND GOLD PLAIN AND CORDED
BRAIDS.

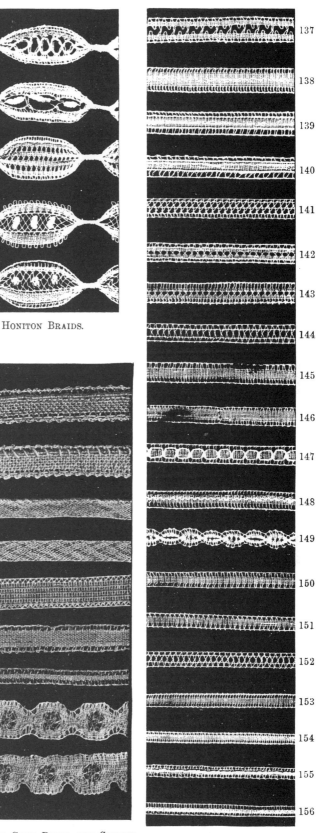

137
138
139
140
141
142
143
144
145
146
147
148
149
150
151
152
153
154
155
156

POINT LACE BRAIDS.

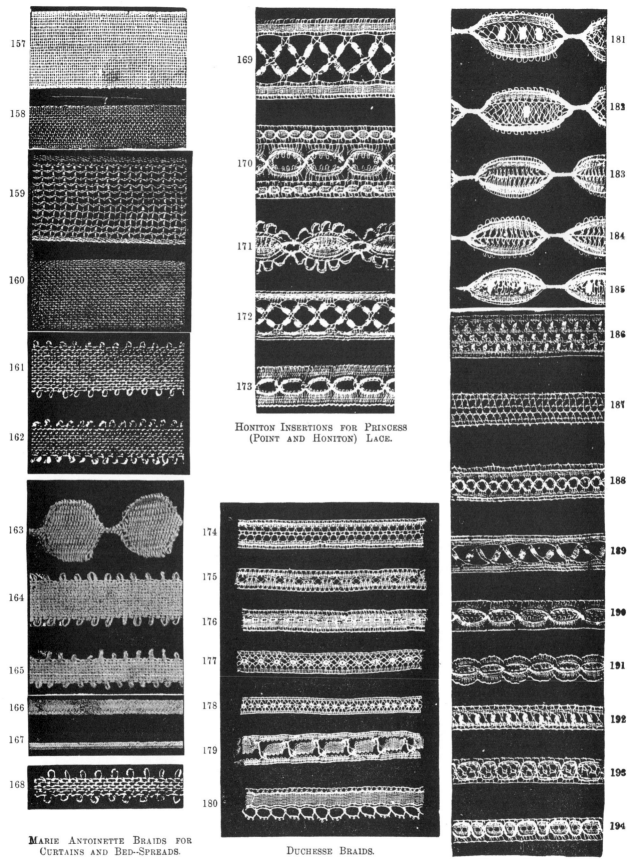

157

158

159

160

161

162

169

170

171

172

173

HONITON INSERTIONS FOR PRINCESS
(POINT AND HONITON) LACE.

163

164

165

166

167

168

MARIE ANTOINETTE BRAIDS FOR
CURTAINS AND BED-SPREADS.

174

175

176

177

178

179

180

DUCHESSE BRAIDS.

181

182

183

184

185

186

187

188

189

190

191

192

193

194

HONITON INSERTIONS.

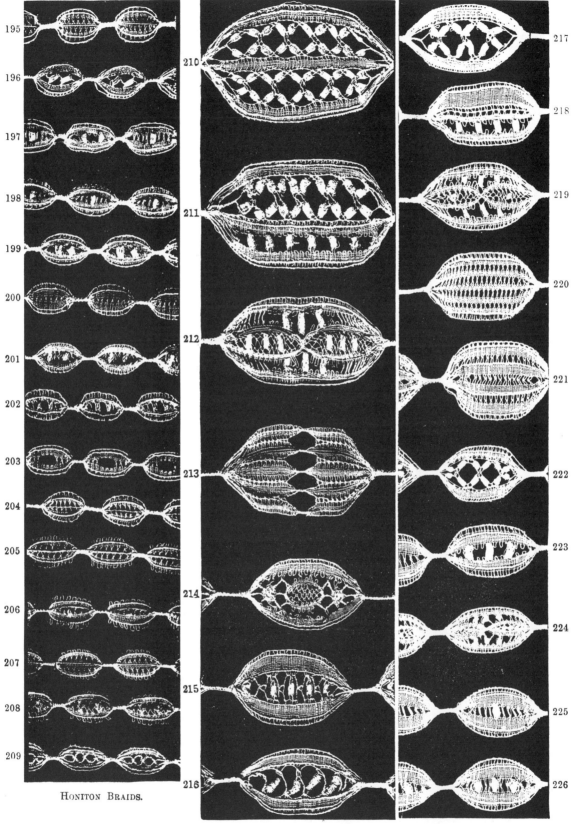

195
196
197
198
199
200
201
202
203
204
205
206
207
208
209

HONITON BRAIDS.

210
211
212
213
214
215
216

IDEAL HONITON BRAIDS.

217
218
219
220
221
222
223
224
225
226

IDEAL HONITON BRAIDS.

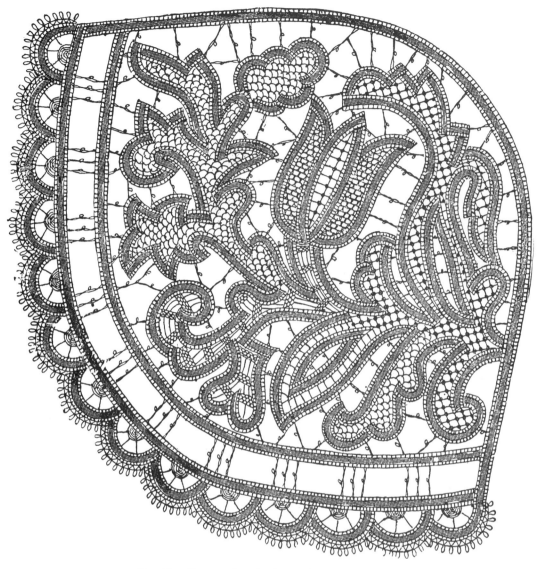

No. 92. —Side of Child's Cap in Battenberg Lace.

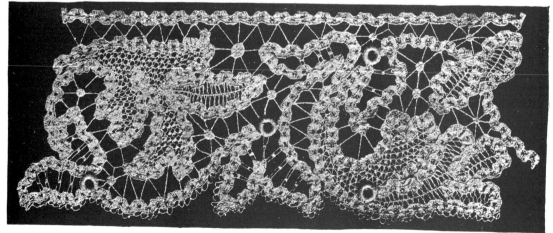

No. 93. —Cluny Lace of Fancy Braid.

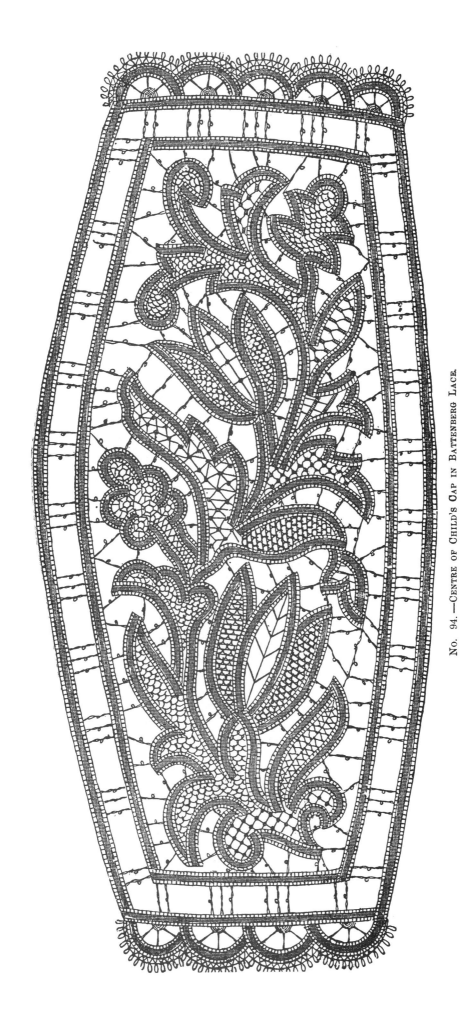

No. 94.—Centre of Child's Oap in Battenberg Lace.

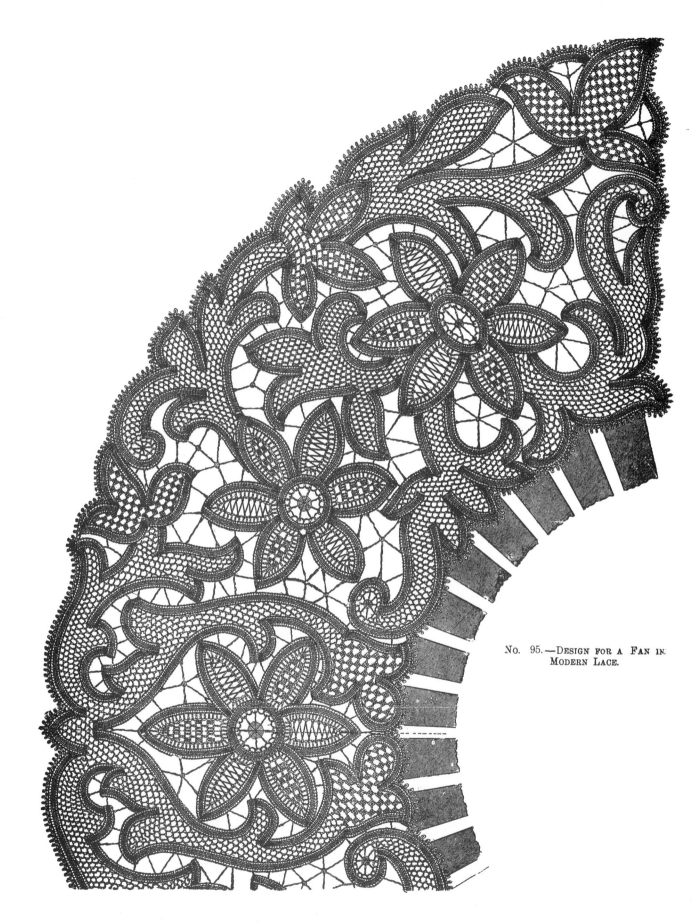

No. 95.—Design for a Fan in Modern Lace.

No. 96.—LADIES' WAIST IN MODERN LACE   (FRONT.)

No. 97.—LACE BUTTERFLY.

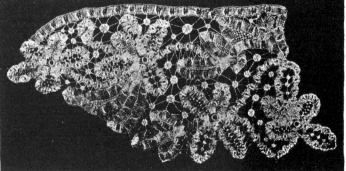

No. 98.—SLEEVE CAP FOR LACE WAIST.

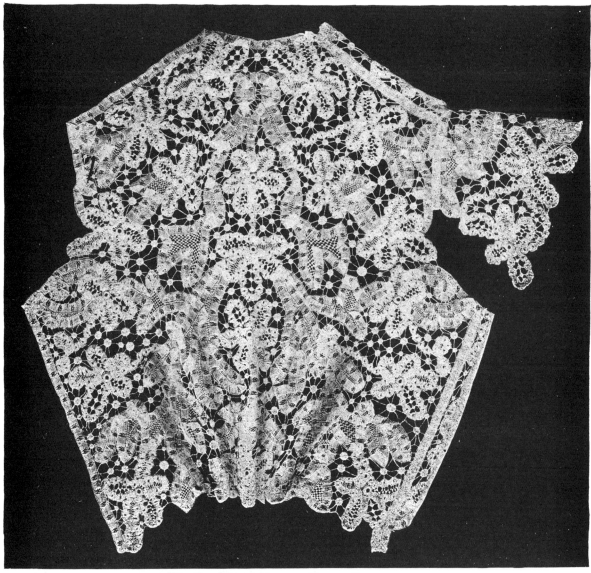

No. 99.—Ladies' Waist in Modern Lace. (Back.)

No. 100.—Modern Lace Edging.

No. 101.—Lace Rose Appliqué.

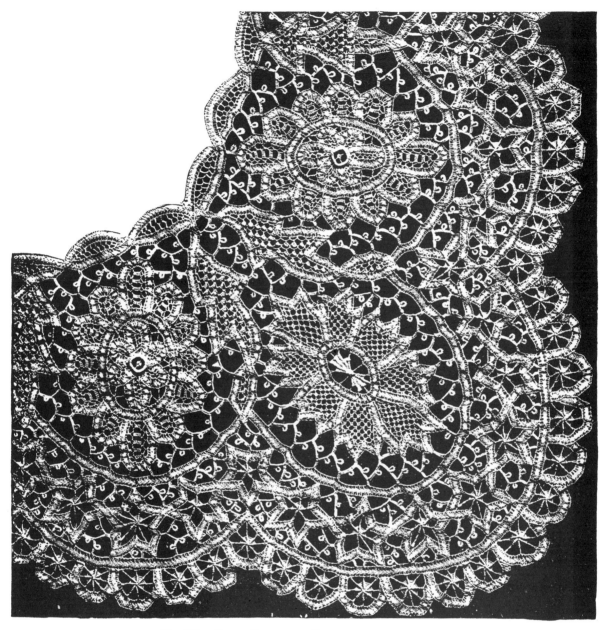

No. 102.—Royal Battenberg Border for Dinner-Cloth.

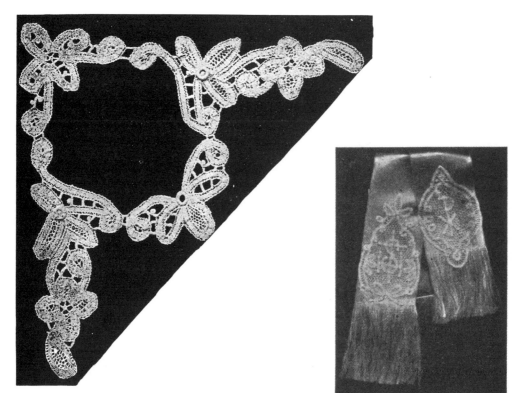

No. 103.—Corner Medallion
for Napkin.

No. 104.—Book-Mark with Point
Lace Medallions.

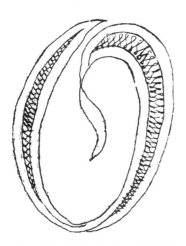

No. 105.—Initial of Lace Braid.

No. 106.—English Point Plate-Doily.

No. 107.—Church Lace of Battenberg.

No. 108.—Altar Lace. (Battenberg.)

No. 109.—Needle Point Lace Barb.

NO. 110.—SCARF-END OF BRUGES LACE.

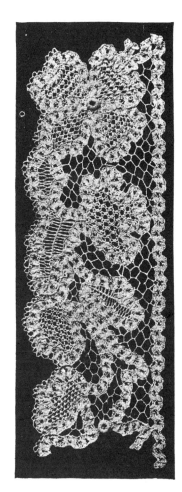

NO. 111.—CLUNY LACE.

No. 112.—VESTIBULE PANEL IN BATTENBERG
LACE.

NO. 113.—POINT LACE FINGER-BOWL DOILY.

79

No. 114. —Insertion for Dinner-Cloth.

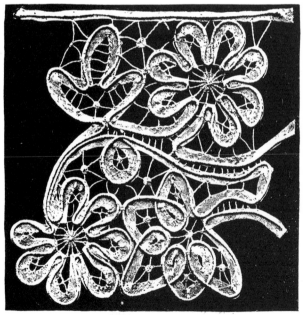

No. 115.—Edging for Dinner-Cloth.

No. 116. —Ladies' Neck-Piece in Modern Lace.

80

No. 117.—Square for Table-Cover in Modern Venetian Point Lace.

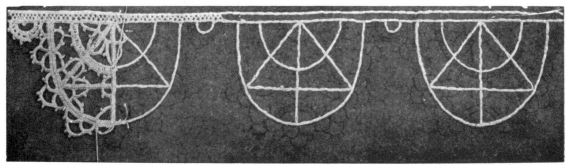

No. 118.—Detail of Modern Venetian Point Lace.

No. 119.—Modern Venetian Point Table-Cover.

(For a Description of this Cover and the Various Purposes for which it is Intended see Pages 7 and 8.)

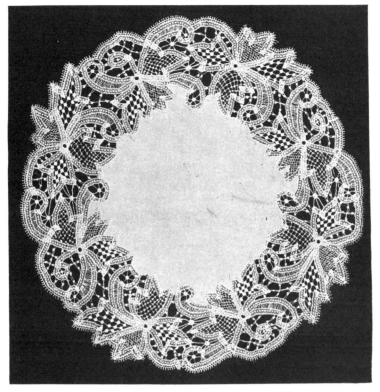

No. 120.—Plate–Doily of English Point Lace.

No. 121.—Net Scarf with Point Lace End.

No. 122.—Watch-Pocket of Modern Lace.

No. 123.—Photograph Frame in Modern Lace.

No. 124.—Chalice Veil.

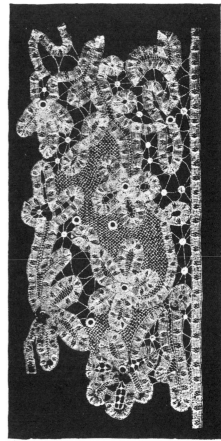

No. 125.—Modern Lace Edging.

No. 126.—Lamp Shade of Satin and Battenberg Lace.

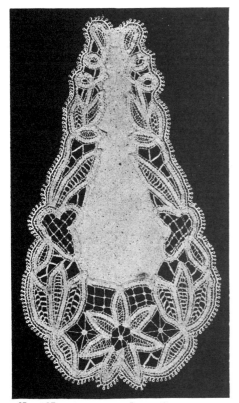

No. 127.—Section of Lamp Shade with Battenberg Border.

No. 128.—Finger-Bowl Doily of Point Lace.

No. 129.—Vestibule Curtain of Marie Antoinette Lace.

No. 130.—Point Lace Collar with Fancy Braid.

No. 131.—Design for
Straight Collar of
Battenberg Lace.

No. 132.—Stock Collar of Russian Lace.

No. 133.—Russian Lace Sleeve to Match
Stock Collar.

No 134.—Modern Point Lace Punch-Glass Doily.

No. 135.—Modern Lace Turn-Over Collar.

No. 136.—Point and Honiton Scarf.   No. 137.—Tie-End in Modern Lace.

No. 138.—Afternoon Tea-Cloth of Flemish Design.

No. 139.—Net Scarf in Modern Lace.

No. 140.—Battenberg Doily.

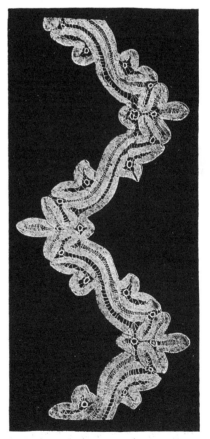

No. 141.—Vandyke Renaissance
Trimming.

89

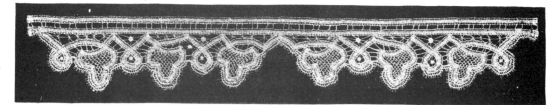

No. 142.—LADIES' POINT LACE TURN-OVER COLLAR.

No. 143.—PRINCESS LACE HANDKERCHIEF.

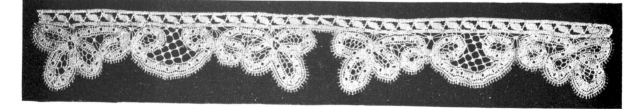

No. 144.—TURN-OVER COLLAR OF BRUGES LACE.

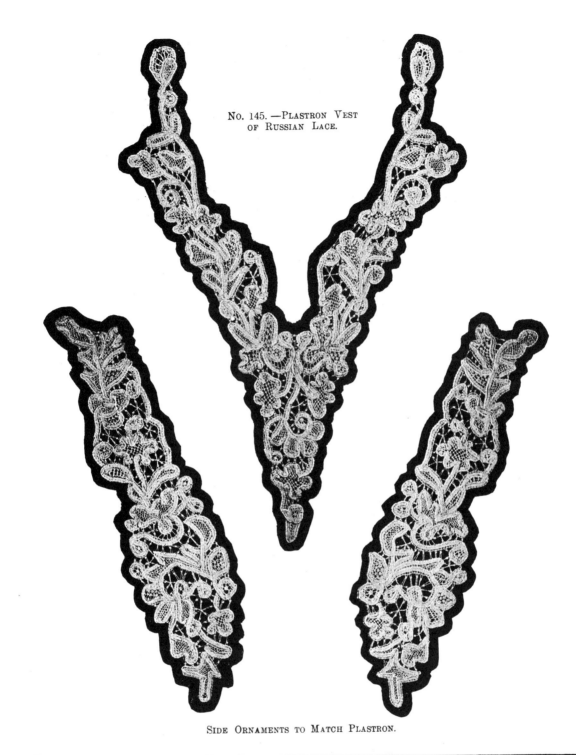

No. 145. —Plastron Vest
of Russian Lace.

Side Ornaments to Match Plastron.

No. 146. —Honiton Lace Turn-Over Collar.

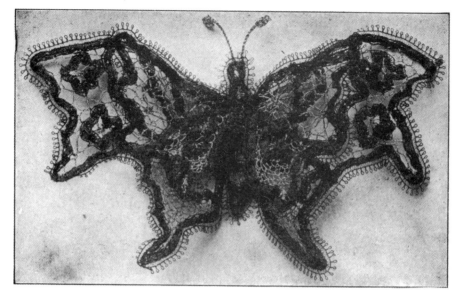

No. 147.—Double Butterfly in Black and Gilt.

No. 148.—Lace End for Ribbon Tie.

No. 149. —Doily of Battenberg Lace (Full Size).

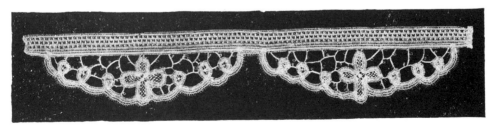

No. 150. —Turn-Over Collar of Modern Lace.

No. 151.—Sofa-Pillow in Honiton Appliqué.

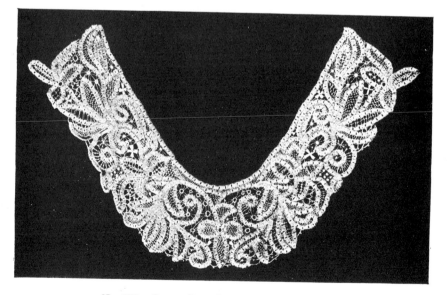

No. 152.—Cream Silk Collar in Modern Lace.

No. 153.—HANDKERCHIEF WITH NEEDLE POINT BORDER.

No. 154.—RENAISSANCE
INSERTION.

No. 155.—DUCHESSE LACE EDGING.

95

No. 156.—DESIGN FOR A BUTTERFLY IN POINT LACE.

No. 157.—INSERTION FOR DINNER-CLOTH.

No. 158.—LACE EDGE FOR DINNER-CLOTH.

No. 159.—Flounce in Bruges Lace (One-Half the Actual Width).

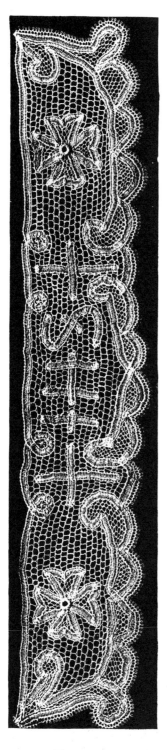

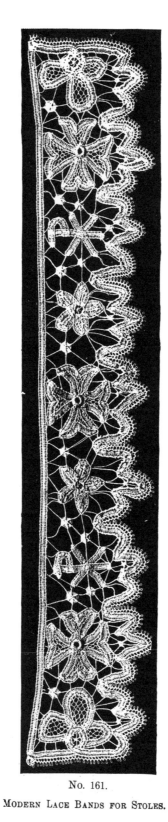

No. 160.   No. 161.   No. 162.

MODERN LACE BANDS FOR STOLES.

98

No. 163.—Renaissance Insertion.

No. 164.—Renaissance Edging.

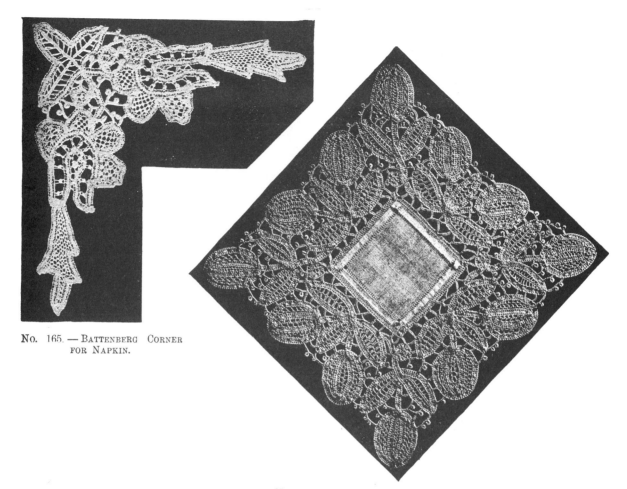

No. 165. — Battenberg Corner
for Napkin.

No. 166. — Battenberg Lace Finger-Bowl Doily.

No. 167. — Handkerchief with Honiton Border.

No. 168. — Rose Point Lace Tie.

No. 169.—Design in Honiton Lace.

No. 170.—"Cardinal's Point" Lace.

101

No. 171.—Handkerchief of Princess Lace.

No. 172.—Double Butterfly of Modern Lace.

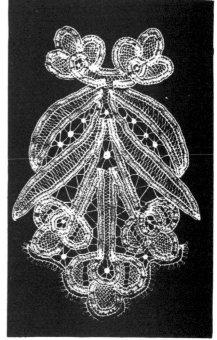

No. 173.—Point Lace Tie-End.

102

No. 174.—Modern Flemish Lace Flounce.

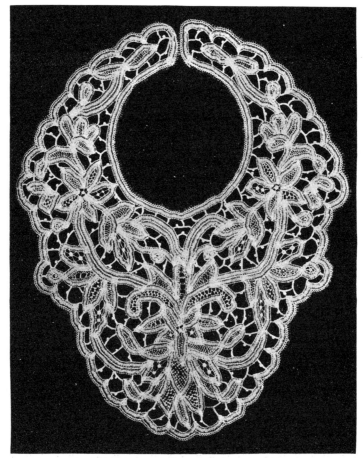

No. 175.—Infants' Bib in Battenberg Lace.

No. 176.—Handkerchief Corner in Honiton and Point.

No. 177.—Point Lace Collar and Cuff.

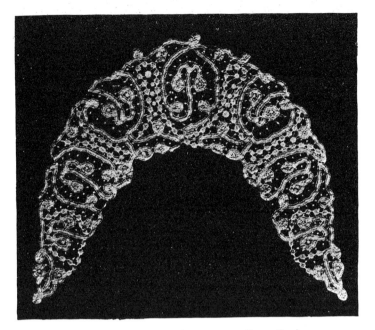

No. 178.—COLLAR OF HONITON AND POINT LACE.

No. 179.—LACE EDGING.

No. 180.—CORNER OF POINT LACE, FOR HANDKERCHIEFS, DOILIES, ETC.

No. 181.—Butterfly of English Point.

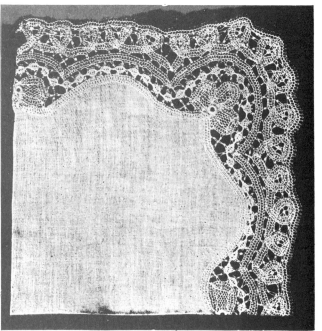

No. 182.—Princess Lace Handkerchief.

No. 183.—Princess Lace Flounce.

No. 184.—Turn-Over Collar
formed of Star Braid.

No. 185.—Sherbet Doily
of Modern Lace.

No. 186.—Design for Carriage Parasol Cover
of Battenberg Lace.

No. 187.—Modern Lace Edge.

No. 188.—Handkerchief in Needle Point.

108

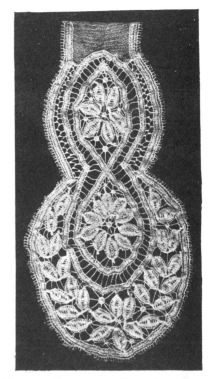

No. 190.—Honiton and Point Lace Barb.

No. 191.—Point Lace Handkerchief.

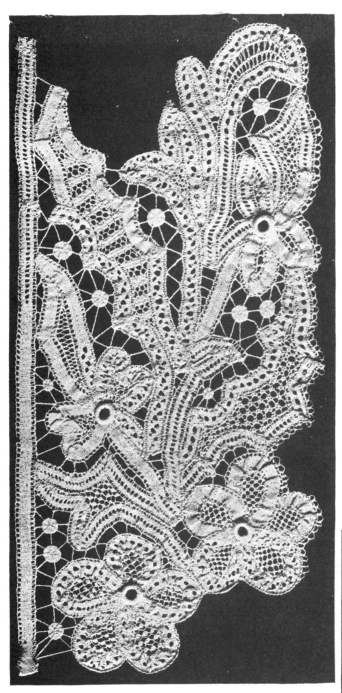

No. 189.—Cluny Lace Flounce.

No. 192.—Sherbet Doily in Princess Lace.

APPENDIX.

DESIGNS FOR BOLEROS, WAIST SETS, DRESS TRIMMINGS, ETC.

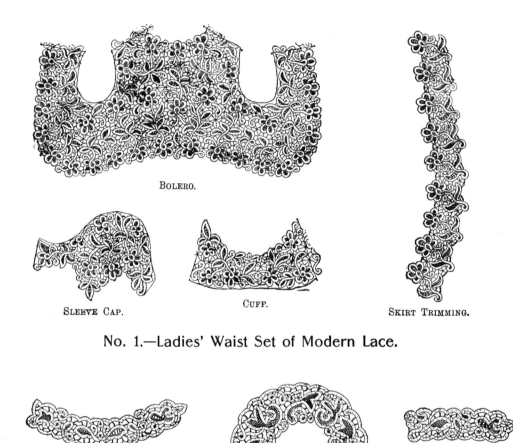

BOLERO.

SLEEVE CAP.

CUFF.

SKIRT TRIMMING.

No. 1.—Ladies' Waist Set of Modern Lace.

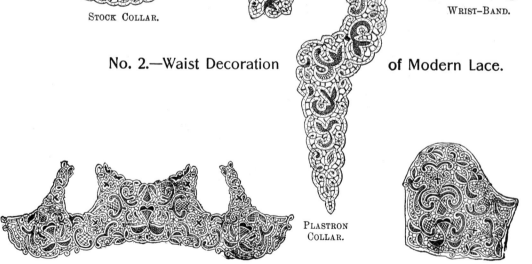

STOCK COLLAR.

WRIST-BAND.

No. 2.—Waist Decoration of Modern Lace.

PLASTRON COLLAR.

No. 3.—Ladies' Lace Bolero and Half Sleeve.

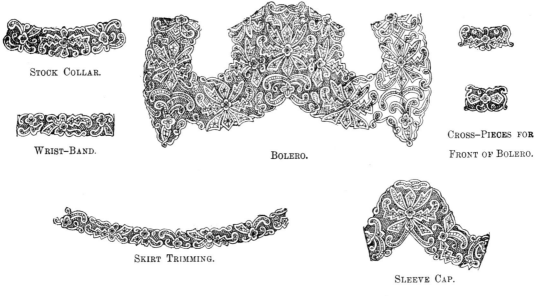

STOCK COLLAR.

WRIST-BAND.

BOLERO.

CROSS-PIECES FOR
FRONT OF BOLERO.

SKIRT TRIMMING.

SLEEVE CAP.

No. 4.—Ladies' Waist Set of Modern Lace.

No. 5.—Ladies' Lace Bolero and Half Sleeve.

No. 6.—Set of Medallions in Modern Lace for Skirt or Waist Decoration.

111